FAMILY CARS
TRIGGER MEMOIRS

FAMILY CARS TRIGGER MEMOIRS

Write your memoirs by thinking small! Share your life experiences before they are lost!

DR. H. KENNETH SHOOK

iUniverse, Inc.
Bloomington

Family Cars Trigger Memoirs
Write your memoirs by thinking small! Share your life experiences before they are lost!

iUniverse books may be ordered through booksellers or by contacting:

iUniverse
1663 Liberty Drive
Bloomington, IN 47403
www.iuniverse.com
1-800-Authors (1-800-288-4677)

Because of the dynamic nature of the Internet, any web addresses or links contained in this book may have changed since publication and may no longer be valid. The views expressed in this work are solely those of the author and do not necessarily reflect the views of the publisher, and the publisher hereby disclaims any responsibility for them.

Any people depicted in stock imagery provided by Thinkstock are models, and such images are being used for illustrative purposes only.
Certain stock imagery © Thinkstock.

ISBN: 978-1-4759-0805-3 (sc)
ISBN: 978-1-4759-0807-7 (hc)
ISBN: 978-1-4759-0806-0 (ebk)

Library of Congress Control Number: 2012905741

Printed in the United States of America

iUniverse rev. date: 04/26/2012

QUOTATIONS ON GETTING HOOKED
ON MEMOIRS

"Your story of Robert Frost's visit to the Wesleyan campus in 1953 is heartwarming and memorable, and it must become part of the Wesleyan Archives." <u>Suzy Taraba</u>, Un. Archivist

"Love your songs, but it was the memoir of your 1992 Rotary visit to New Zealand that I enjoyed the most." <u>Glenn Estess, Sr.</u>, Past Rotary International President

I read "the Athletics Newsletter with its delightful memoir of spring training in Frederick. I knew I'd like it, and I did." (1/30/09) Thanks for "the delightful account of your phone calls with Kelly and ambidextrous Greg Harris. It's warm and unusual material, very American." (5/07/09) "I loved your piece about the Methodist boy holding a baby for the Pope. It amply justifies my thesis—and yours—that no amount of invention can beat what people actually do; the truth is endlessly surprising and absorbing. The fact that you per-severed in tracking down the photographer after 45 years is equally unexpected and gives the story a satisfying credibility."(7/15/09) <u>William Zinsser</u>—Author and Educator

Thanks for the song "My Pre-Game Routine." "I always enjoy taking a look back at my career and remembering all the pre-game rituals." (8/09/06) <u>Cal Ripken, Jr.</u>

The 1960s Training Camps *"were special days with special people, the team, the fans"*—Baltimore Colt <u>Raymond Berry</u>

Words of Thanks and Photograph Sources

As stated in my first memoir book, *Getting Hooked on Memoirs,* I again extend thanks to the many people who offered me encouragement as they listened to my memoirs and responded to the stories I shared at memoir workshops and book fairs. In addition, I especially thank William Zinsser, noted author and educator, for his numerous phone conversations and his letters that I highly treasure. Kind words were received from Raymond and Sally Berry, Greg and Kelly Harris, and also the families of Rotary International Presidents Kalyan and Binota Banerjee, Luis and Celia Giay, and Raja and Usha Saboo. Helpful advice also came to me from Suzanna Tamminen, Director of the Wesleyan University Press, and thanks to Mary Lou Martin for manuscript editing.

Photograph acknowledgements: Some photographers of pictures are identified in the book as the photos are used, but nearly all are our own products. On page 29, Ed Holl and Ward Shoemaker photos come from a Madison High yearbook of 1958. On page 48, my family photo was used in a 1970s Westminster Methodist Church Directory. On page 88, Bob Fowler took the photo of his mother-in-law's party. On page 96, the Plymouth photo was provided by my daughter, Jennette Reynolds, and finally, the two Harris photos on page 142 were given by Kelly and Greg Harris.

AN AUTHOR'S APPROACH TO
MEMOIR WRITING

It is my opinion that every book or collection of memoirs needs an introductory statement which clearly states the author's ground rules. This approach would correspond to the pre-game routine conducted prior to most athletic events. The umpire or game official calls the team captains together and discusses rules and special conditions that apply to that event. Memoir writers need to do the same thing. I wrote my first memoir in 2003, and, prior to putting my words on paper, I had surveyed much of the material written on the topic of memoirs. I admit to you that the term "memoir" means different things to different people, and it seems that each writer is allowed to put his or her own spin on the topic. My thoughts and conclusions were rather well formed when I came in contact with articles and books written by William Zinsser. The writings of this educator and author convinced me that my thoughts on memoir writing were on the right track, and I have often stated that Zinsser's best advice on writing memoirs is to "Think small!"

By the year 2005, my willingness to "think small" had allowed me to produce some seventy memoirs that dealt with a wide array of memorable happenings in my life. At some point, I would follow another of Mr. Zinsser's suggestions. I would spread the memoirs out on the living room rug to study the best ways to arrange them into meaningful categories. When you do begin grouping your memoirs, you'll find it takes a lot of thought, because each memoir has the potential to belong to numerous groups. The year 2005 was also the year that I began conducting sessions on writing and sharing memoirs. In those workshops, I shared my knowledge on the topic as we sought answers to the following basic questions: 1) What is a memoir? 2) Does it have a desired length? 3) Should the details of the writer's experience or happening be true? 4) Could the writer be sharing the experiences of others rather than his own experiences? 5) How does a memoir differ from a research paper? 6) How does it differ from a complete life-history? 7) Should the writing be directed toward a certain audience, such as the writer's own children and grandchildren? 8) Could the topics of memoirs include events of recent weeks or months and not focus solely on events of the distant past? 9) Could writers of memoirs be teenagers rather than senior citizens? 10) Could memoir topics include happenings that many people have experienced and not be limited to "once-in-a-lifetime" experiences?

I view a memoir as an effort on the part of an individual to share a meaningful experience with another person or group. Often the memoir takes the form of a short story with a beginning, middle, and an ending. The middle section would most often describe the memorable event or happening. The beginning would explain why the writer was present and it sets the stage. The ending would point out the results caused by the event and it makes known the impact on the writer or speaker. When possible, the story details should be restricted to a rather narrow span of time which covers the event, and the author's thinking during that time-period could be a vital part of the narrative.

The memoir could be as short as a page or two in length, and photographs and sketches could often enhance the presentation. The event could take place in a few minutes, but it could also be much longer in time. The longer the time-frame, however, the more likely it becomes a life-history rather than classified as a memoir. The memoir event should be the writer's own personal experience, and the details should be true as best the author can recall them. Memoir topics need not be limited to rare events that defy logic and approach the unbelievable, and they should not be research papers. Finally, my memoirs are written to be shared with everyone and not limited in their use to just entertain family members and friends.

My first memoir book, *Getting Hooked on Memoirs*, was written with certain goals in mind. I hoped to generate in readers a sincere interest in memoirs and also to motivate everyone to preserve and share their precious life experiences. Those same goals apply to book two. All of my memoirs are true accounts of my life, exactly as I remember them, and I enjoy sharing the accounts with interested others. My first book offered me an opportunity to share a number of my memoirs with others, but I admitted at that time that my preference was to relate my life experience orally rather than in writing. Facing the audience and sensing their reactions to my story provided me with the greatest satisfaction, one not gained by publishing a book.

As I stated in my first book, only a few of my memoirs qualify as once-in-a-lifetime happenings. It is fine to write a memoir about an experience that others have also shared, such as buying penny candy or buying that first new car. It need not be a unique happening. The interesting people you describe as having an influence on your life need not be celebrities or winners of a Pulitzer Prize. At times, my memoirs are structured to follow a chronological pattern, but even then, each memoir should have a stand-alone capability. Memoirs written by you and other readers could date back to your childhood and your other memoirs could focus on events as recent as last week. A Peanuts cartoon had Snoopy the Dog typing memoirs while seated on top of his dog house. Trying to remember old happenings, Snoopy wrote "What I remember about last week . . . ."

My book, *Family Cars Trigger Memoirs,* was originally designed to have only one theme, but later expanded to three. All memoirs would have been in some way related to family cars. The episodes in this book are all true life experiences, and at times, the events are allowed to merge rather than stand alone as isolated happenings. In this regard, the new style parallels to a degree the single memoir book written by Lawrence Block, his book titled, *Step by Step.* In his book, Block discusses his love for marathons and his travels to various race locations are not intended to be stand-alone episodes. Block writes that his travels are dictated by his desire to enter numerous marathons in all regions of the United States, stopping only long enough to earn some needed money by writing another best-selling novel. Each chapter of his book logically leads to the next chapter. In my case, my opening theme became the title of the book, and family cars do in fact generate most of the memoirs of the book. Distant travels trigger memoirs in this book as they did in my earlier book, *Getting Hooked on Memoirs.* My final theme, namely, *Memoirs Generate Other Memoirs*, allows me to evaluate my success to date in motivating others to share and preserve their life experiences. William Zinsser, noted educator and writer, employs a single theme in his memoir book, *Writing Places,* in which he describes the various locations he used to write his highly successful books on the art of good writing. You would be wise to add these books by Block and Zinsser to your reading list.

As you generate your list of events which have the potential to become future memoirs, remember to think small. I hope you find my memoir material helpful and interesting and that you begin recording and sharing your own life's memorable experiences. To delay this undertaking could cause your worthwhile memories to be lost forever.

Seven Key Steps In Memoir Writing

1. First, generate a list of memorable life experiences, and help it to grow in size.
2. Select a few that are most worthy, and type at least two pages about each event.
3. Put completed memoirs aside before polishing them and checking spelling, etc.
4. As your list of topics grows and weeks pass, return to polish some earlier writings.
5. When your polished memoirs reach 40 or more, spread them out on the living room rug, and try to group them into categories.
6. By now, you should be sharing your polished memoirs with others, even groups.
7. When you share your memoirs with groups and you could hear a pin drop, then consider having your memoirs published.

CONTENTS

PART I

FAMILY CARS TRIGGER MEMOIRS

PART I - FAMILY CARS TRIGGER MEMOIRS

AUTOS IN THE EARLY YEARS (1930-1959):

If my memory of trivia is anywhere near correct, I recall it being said that each person in the United States can expect to live in ten different homes in a lifetime, and each can expect to encounter a dozen or more family cars. For me, I have lived in eight different homes, excluding college dormitories and army barracks. Counting family cars is a more difficult task for me, but if I include the favorite cars owned by my father and my wife's father, my total number of family cars would reach 17. Since I lay no claim to being a "car person," I wonder what the statistics would be for persons who really love cars. My son-in-law, Rob Reynolds, may have an answer to this question in his memoir in Part III of this book.

BEFORE I LEARNED TO DRIVE A CAR:

My father loved Cadillac cars

In my list of family cars, the first was a Cadillac car owned by my father. We lived at 213 East Patrick Street in Frederick, Maryland, which also happened to be my first home. Dad must have had a love for Cadillac cars, because those were the model cars that he selected to restore to perfect riding conditions. Being a skilled mechanic, he could provide us with an expensive looking family car which did not come with a high price tag. Dad was a farm boy in his youth, and his education was often disrupted by farm chores and other family duties. For this reason, he lacked a high school diploma, and his employment as a mechanic, as a road construction foreman, and as a policeman would cause our family to warrant a low-income label.

Mother, on the other hand, had a college degree from Hood College, located in Frederick, but her college education never led to full-time employment outside the

3

home. Her contributions of cooking, sewing, and piano playing were valuable assets to our family, and it should be remembered that the decision to be a stay-at-home mom was a prevailing opinion until the cultural changes that were brought about by World War II. Brother Charlie and I learned at an early age that we needed to provide most of our own spending money, and we sometimes held two or three jobs, especially if our goal was to purchase a special item, such as a ball glove or gifts to give others at Christmas time. Our younger sister, Kathy, did not make her appearance until 1947, seventeen years after my birth, so she was not part of these early Shook memoirs. Also, we had a step-brother, Herman, born on March 1, 1920. For a variety of reasons, Herman's impact on my life did not seem to begin until he entered the military in World War II, and he was in our thoughts as he served a number of years overseas, stationed in England.

Uncle Percy and the milk truck event

For a number of years, Dad did work part-time for my uncle, Percy Beavers, driving trucks to out of state locations, and sometimes Charlie or I joined Dad when the destination was Scranton, PA. The truck was carrying a large number of milk containers, and I could lift the metal cans only if they were empty of milk. On one long trip that I did not make with Dad, Uncle Percy did decide to accompany him. Dad did not trust Mr. Beavers as a driver, because he had been known to fall asleep at the wheel. Nevertheless, on that particular return trip from Scranton, Mr. Beavers insisted on driving, and Dad consented. Dad tried to take a short nap, but that almost resulted in a disaster. When Dad opened his eyes, they were crossing a bridge on the edge of a small town, and the truck was headed toward the bridge railing. Uncle Percy had fallen asleep. Dad quickly grabbed the wheel and yanked it 90 degrees, turning back toward the road. The truck did not go over the side of the bridge, but it flipped onto its side, and the top fell off, causing all contents to spill out on to the highway. At 3:00 in the morning, at least one hundred large milk cans banged and rolled their way across the bridge, waking up all of the residents of that sleepy town. Out in the road, Dad was concerned about the disturbance, but he also worried that the truck might catch on fire. When Mr. Beavers was nowhere to be found outside the truck, Dad finally found him, still moving around in the cab of the truck. Dad hollered for him to get out of the truck, fearing that a truck fire was a possibility. Percy called back to Dad: "I'm trying to find my hat."

These singing brothers were popular

My own memory of life events seems to start in 1934 when I was just four years of age. At that age, I began singing duets with my brother Charlie, two years my senior. Charlie sang the melody line of songs, mainly hymns, and, somehow, I produced the words by watching his lips. At the same time, I harmonized by generating a tenor flow of notes even though I could not read the notes printed on the pages of music and no one had taught me how to harmonize. We are pictured below, and in the photo next to us is our father in his police uniform.

My brother and I sang the well-known hymn *Have Thine own way, Lord!* hundreds of times in the 1930s, and that was one song in our music repertoire that I did not need to read my brother's lips to acquire the song's lyrics. The first verse lyrics were:

> Have Thine own way, Lord! Have Thine own way!
> Thou art the Potter, I am the clay.
> Mold me and make me after Thy will,
> While I am waiting, yielded and still.

Charlie and I, our parents, and our family car were all kept busy fulfilling invitations to perform at numerous churches, granges, the local WFMD radio station, the Odd Fellows Home, family reunions, retirement homes, and Frederick City music talent shows. Some of these events took place at the band pavilion in Frederick City's Baker Park and others were held on the stage of the beautiful Tivoli Theater. Audiences loved the hymns we sang, like *Have Thine Own Way, Lord*, and the humorous songs that we sang. One humorous song, *Get Away Old Man, Get Away,* never failed to produce laughter and applause. The words to the old folk song went something like this:

> *Don't ever marry an ole man, I'll tell you the reason why.*
> *His lips are all tobacco juice, and his chin is never dry. (Chorus)*
> *I'd rather marry a young man with his pockets lined with silk than to marry an ole man with a hundred cows to milk. (Chorus)*

*I'd rather have a young man with an apple
in his hand than to have an ole man with a
hundred acres of land. (Chorus)
Chorus: For an ole man he is old, and an ole
man he is gray, but a young man's heart is
full of love. Get away, ole man! Get away!*

My mother frequently told the story of one singing engagement that my brother Charlie wished all would forget. Mother's version of the happening related that she played the introduction to one of our songs and Charlie failed to sing, so she repeated the introduction. She knew that I followed Charlie's lead, often reading his lips to acquire the words to the song. Although my reading skills were apparently limited at age four, I could vocalize a tenor harmony while Charlie sang the song's melody. I must have been frustrated with my brother, because I hit him and said aloud: "Sing, Charles! Sing! "The audience of over 100 people saw great humor in the situation, but Charlie told me later of his great embarrassment. He claims he had a mental blank that night, and he had to walk over to the piano to check on the words. Some say that I kicked Charlie to get his attention, but Charlie says he remembers it as a poke in the ribs with my elbow.

Parking downtown on Saturday nights

In June of 1936, I was only six years old, but I vividly remember a typical Saturday night when we parked the family car on North Market Street in Frederick, our home town. On that night, we secured our favorite parking spot in front of the White Star Restaurant which sold the best hot dogs in town. The habit of parking the family car on a main city street on a Saturday night to socialize and watch people stroll past was a habit found in many small towns in the 1930s and early 1940s.

There were no parking meters to contend with in the 1940s, and television had not yet become a force to keep people at home in their living rooms. Frederick stores were delighted to see the sidewalks filled with potential customers, and farm families viewed the weekends as their best chance to see friends in town and to do the weekly shopping. Our choice parking spot in Frederick was just a few doors from the Square Corner, the intersection of Patrick Street and Market Street. Market Street ran north and south, and Patrick Street ran east and west, and these two streets still allowed driving in both directions. Years later, when Market Street was made into a one-way street going north, Dad was on police duty at the Square Corner when he saw an elderly gent attempting to make a U-turn, about to drive his car in the wrong direction on Market Street. Dad called out: "Frank, you can't turn around there!" The old fellow continued to turn toward the south as he called back: "Don't worry, Denver, I can make it." Dad claims that he got to laughing so hard that he failed to chase after the car that was headed into "one-way" traffic.

On one typical Saturday night in June of 1936, we parked in our choice location, and on that particular night, Joe Lewis just happened to be fighting the German boxer Max Schmeling in the famous Yankee Stadium. Although the fight was sold out, sports fans were able to listen to the radio broadcast of the Arthur Donovan officiated fight. Some fans were, no doubt, aware of the racial issues involved in the outcome of the fight, and others may have been thinking about Hitler and his push for power in Germany. I heard a radio playing in the middle of the block, and after each round of the fight I relayed the results back to the family car. As best I can remember, I played a neutral role that night, as would any sports announcer seeking to be fair to each fighter. Sometimes I reported that Schmeling was coming on strong, and sometimes I mentioned that Lewis landed strong blows in certain rounds. The event scheduled for fifteen rounds ended in round twelve, when Schmeling won by a knockout. The outcome of the fight was met by mixed reactions, but those near our parked car seemed to appreciate my efforts to deliver the round-by-round coverage. My reward was a White Star hot dog with all the trimmings, and I know that I had no trouble falling asleep after that busy Saturday night.

Because of this experience in 1936, I followed the careers of Schmeling and Lewis over many decades, and I learned to admire and respect the German fighter Schmeling. After losing to Lewis in their final boxing match, he continued to visit Lewis in the United States, and when Lewis was on hard times, he often gave Lewis money to cover some of his debts. When Lewis died on April 12, 1981, it was reported that Schmeling served as a pallbearer and paid the Lewis funeral expenses.

Sunday drives and Burma Shave signs

A favorite memory of my childhood was the "Sunday drive." In the 1930s and early-1940s, the family car took us to church in the morning, and in the afternoon we would visit relatives or simply enjoy driving the country roads. The country roads in those days were usually two-lanes wide, sometimes making it difficult to pass a slow moving car or farm vehicle. On occasion, we even had to come to a complete stop to allow herds of cattle to cross the road to enter another field. My home was in Frederick County, Maryland, and in that dairy and farming community even the farmers viewed Sundays as a day of rest. Many amusements were not open to the public on Sundays in these years, such as: movie houses, golf courses, department stores, and skating rinks. Also, there were no shopping malls to visit. If our drives encountered bad weather, Charlie and I could sleep on the back seat of the family car, knowing that Dad would be able to cope with ice and snow and foggy windows, getting us safely home. Another bad weather problem resulted from my father's enjoyment of White Owl cigars. When he smoked them while the car windows were closed, breathing in the back seat became difficult. In good weather, windows remained open to the fresh air.

On Sunday drives my brother Charlie and I enjoyed looking for road signs, especially those known as Burma Shave signs. These signs were a novel idea which apparently saved the Burma Shave Company from failure. The signs required that five or six posters be placed on the same number of polls, and the short jingles were often fun to read while driving down the road. I collected a sampling of the jingles in 1972 when I served as President of the Westminster Rotary Club. Each time I told a joke or read a jingle, club members would drop silverware on the floor, an indication that they wanted even more of my humor. Most of the jingles I shared with Rotarians and some that they shared with me must have been Burma Shave originals, but others could have been imposters. Some of those favorite jingles, with the "Burma Shave!" endings deleted, were:

> A peach looks good with lots of fuzz, but man's no peach and never was.
> Don't stick your elbow out so far. It might go home in another car.
> Her chariot raced at eighty per. They hauled away what had Ben-Hur.
> The monkey took one look at Jim, and threw the peanuts back at him.
> Dinah doesn't treat him right, but if he'd shave, Dyna-mite!
> Ben met Anna, made a hit. Neglected beard, Ben-Anna split!

Rare visits to the ball park

On a limited number of occasions, our Dad might drive us in the family car to Washington, DC, to see a major league baseball game, or he might possibly drive us to Baltimore to visit relatives. These two-hour round trips were not typical "Sunday drives." Our cousins, Bobby and Amon Burgee, lived in Baltimore, and all of us boys loved to play ball whenever we got together. These cousins joined us at least once on our visit to Griffith Stadium, the home of the Washington Senators. One such memorable game was a contest with the Boston Red Sox, and all eyes were on Boston's Ted Williams, one of the greatest hitters to ever play the game. He did hit a home run that day, but several other long drives were caught before they could land in the bleachers. It seems hard to believe, but parking space for the Senator fans was mainly limited to street parking, and the stadium resembled a drab factory. What was attractive was the playing field, and many youngsters dreamed of playing there someday. My dreams were not unlike those of other youngsters, but I knew that dreams often do not become realities.

LEARNING TO DRIVE AND RECEIVING MY LICENSE:

My step-brother's Nash coop in 1946

As stated earlier, my brother Charlie and I had a step-brother named Herman. In the early-1940s photo shown below Herman is pictured in military uniform. Charlie and I are kneeling, and mother and dad are

standing. Herman's entry into the service in World War II was the event that seemed to bring him into my life and into my thinking. I do remember the War years, listening to President Roosevelt tell of the Japanese attack of Pearl Harbor in December of 1941, but Herman serving in the Air Force in England during World War II was what generated great interest in news reports in the Shook household. In prior years, he seldom if ever stayed with us in our 213 East Patrick Street home in

11

Frederick, and I can only guess that he lived much of those earlier years with his real mother in Thurmont, MD. If my limited knowledge was correct, prior to 1940, some major friction apparently existed between Dad and Herman, and I sense that those conditions made it difficult for Herman to adjust to Dad's second marriage and also to adjust to Herman's second family. I understand that Herman, on a number of occasions, actually ran away from home, which led to disciplinary action which was severe, too severe, in my opinion, for a person of Herman's age.

Whatever problems may have existed in Herman's life prior to 1940, all were gone and forgotten when he returned from England with his war-bride. He met Thomasina in Norwich, and he brought her back to live in Thurmont, Maryland. In adjusting to civilian life, he held a restaurant job, and later, he also worked with a typewriter business and with an insurance firm. Eventually, he found that law enforcement would be his best fit in life, and that became his final career. He became Chief of Police in Thurmont, a job that brought him into contact with US Presidents as they visited near-by Camp David. Herman acquired a Nash coop as his first car after the War, and using that car, he taught me to drive when I turned sixteen. I found the standard shift to be no problem, and even stopping and starting on hills went smoothly.

Herman also gave me my first set of golf clubs, and I often told Herman he was good at teaching me to drive a car but less successful in teaching me to drive a golf ball. Part of the problem may have been that he gave me his old set of clubs, Ken Nagle model clubs. This Australian golfer did win a National Open in 1960, but Nagle's clubs had the smallest club heads I had ever seen, offering a small sweet spot for any beginning golfer. In praise of Herman, he often filled a father role for me that Dad had failed to fill. In my thinking, I wondered why Dad had not attempted to teach me to drive a car. My brother, Charlie, surprised me when he revealed that Dad had actually taught him to drive. Charlie guessed that Dad may have been lonely for some companionship on his drives to and from Brunswick, Maryland, a town where he had started a new garage business. My learning to drive at age sixteen would prove to be a skill that I would not use until age twenty-two, but the absence of a car for those six years never seemed to be a concern of mine.

Viewing the *Duel in the Sun* movie

When a movie is seen repeated times, it tends to remain near the surface of one's memory, thus being an item that is easily recalled. On a very long flight to Singapore in 1998, my wife and I must have viewed the movie *Shakespeare in Love* three or four times, and we enjoyed each and every showing of the film. In 1946, my age was sixteen, and I viewed the film *Duel in the Sun* at least three times on the same day, thanks to my brother's rather unusual employment. Herman had returned home from serving in the military in England in World War II, and a part-time job required him to monitor movie theaters in small Frederick County towns. One of these small towns was Woodsboro, Maryland, if my memory is functioning properly. I always accepted Herman's invitation for me to join him on movie visits. While Herman checked to see that movie patrons equaled the number of tickets sold, I watched the movie that was in progress. While he verified that employees performed their duties and that safety regulations were followed, I watched the movies. The main film was usually shown twice at these weekend events, and between shows, light refreshments could be purchased. It took about ten minutes for the one projector to rewind the film, and during such an interval the typical small town audience had enough time to easily clear the restrooms and return to their folded chairs. The only movie I remember from those small town visits was the highly publicized film *Duel in the Sun*.

The 1946 film *Duel in the Sun* had been buried deep in my memory for better than 50 years, but, for whatever reason, last night it resurfaced and I decided to add it to this memoir. The reason it resurfaced, while other films did not, may be explained by the movie's star-studded cast. Even after these many years, I vividly recall the roles played by Jennifer Jones and Gregory Peck. Jennifer Jones may have gotten an Academy Award that year. I had forgotten that Joseph Cotton also had a role in the movie, but I did remember that the director was David O. Selznick, famous for his direction of the earlier film *Gone with the Wind*. His 1946 film was highly expensive, I recall, and many parts had to be censored for sexual content reasons.

OWNING A LICENSE BUT HAVING NO CAR ACCESS:

As I record my "family car" memoirs, I am quite aware that for some people a family car had not been and would never be a part of their daily lives. This would have been especially true for certain families living in large urban centers. For them, a car could actually be viewed as a burden and parking costs could be excessive. I never lived in large cities, but I too had a period in my life when I possessed a driver's license but had no access to a car. For this reason, I decided to add a number of memoirs which were triggered not by the presence of the family car but by the absence of such a car.

One high school classmate had a car

When my driver's license was obtained in 1946, receiving the card in no way changed my daily routine. I continued to use my bicycle to attend school and to perform the duties required by my multiple jobs. No car was ever at my disposal, and while attending high school few classmates were an exception to this pattern. Jock Dixon, one of my closest friends in high school, had no car, but he died when he accepted a ride in a car of another Frederick High student. My memoir about his tragic death appears in my first memoir book, *Getting Hooked on Memoirs*. A number of our classmates had returned from military service, and they were older than the rest of us. One veteran impressed the rest of us as he rode a very large motorcycle to school and he dated the most attractive girls. Another classmate of my own age did have a car for his personal use, and he was a farm boy by the name of Robert Young. For his junior and senior years at Frederick High, I imagined that he had a full social life, dating any girls of interest to him. The car seemed to make the difference. Also, I assumed that well-to-do parents gave him everything he desired, and he most likely had few farm choirs for which he was responsible. Bob was nice looking, I'll give him that, but the availability of the car was what set him apart from most other classmates. At least that is what I thought at the time.

Many years after my graduation from Frederick High School, I returned to Frederick to spend a day at the Great Frederick Fair. This late-September or early-October annual event was something I had enjoyed throughout my entire youth. We actually got a Friday off from school to attend the fair, but I expected to attend every day because my mother worked at the fair. She actually kept all of the official records of the fair, and she recorded the vast amount of material into books by hand. Her work showed flawless penmanship, and no computers were available to do the job in the late-1930s and early-1940s. I enjoyed returning to the fair as an adult, and when not walking through the buildings of arts and crafts and walking the mid-ways, I would watch horse races from the grandstands at the track. On one particular day the person seated directly in front of me in the stands was classmate Bob Young. He and his wife laughed when I shared with them my version of Bob's ownership of a car while still a Frederick High student. Bob's version was quite different from mine, and he asked me "Did you not know why my parents gave me that car to use?" Since I did not know, Bob said that he was kicked off the school bus for a disturbance, and his parents were told that they had to provide Bob's transportation from that point until his graduation. Bob claimed the car was no benefit to his social life in high school, and he insists his farm duties actually increased after the expulsion from the school bus. According to Bob, the car he had in high school was certainly no blessing.

The Charlotte Hall School experience

After my high school graduation in 1947, the discontinuation of my schooling was never a consideration for me, but money problems did exist. A football scholarship seemed certain, provided I started college at Bucknell University in 1948 rather than 1947. A scholarship that was available from the Maryland State Scholarship Board for the academic year 1947-1948 would pay for one year of post-graduate study at the Charlotte Hall School, and a relative of mine just happened to be headmaster at that school. Since Charlotte Hall was located below Washington, DC, in southern Maryland, I would have my first experience living away from home. Dad's car would need to make about four round trips to Charlotte Hall to allow me to attend the school.

Major Miel Burgee, my second-cousin, was head of the school in 1947, and he and wife, Olga, had a home on campus. They had no children, and both were delighted that I would be a Charlotte Hall student. Almost immediately, I suffered a severe injury to my right knee during a football practice and I needed to spend nearly a month in bed to recuperate. Phil Kritzing was the name of the fellow who caused the injury by charging across the line before the signal was given, and he also happened to have graduated with me from Frederick High School in 1947. The persons carrying me off the field that day allowed the leg to twist, causing even greater damage to the right knee. In later years, such a knee injury might have received an immediate operation, but in 1947, I was told that without operating I could regain 80-85% of the use of my right leg. Recovery would not be an easy process. Living in a dorm room would not provide the attention that I needed, so Olga Burgee insisted that I be moved into a bedroom in her home.

My only other injury suffered that year at Charlotte Hall was a tooth broken in a varsity basketball game. The dentist, Dr. Voshell, had his office in La Plata, MD, and my three or four visits cost about $50 in 1948. I was the vocalist for the school dance band at the time, and while I was singing, the wax used to fill the vacant front-tooth position would fly out of my mouth. I learned to catch the wax in air and replace it without missing a note of music. Would you believe me if I told you that the song lyrics *All I want for Christmas is my two front teeth* were first published in 1946? I kid you not!

My dental visits to La Plata required the use of a Charlotte Hall school van, and buses owned by the school were available to transport the basketball and baseball teams on which I played. My other needs for transportation vehicles included the need for a bike, to aid in the rehabilitation of my injured knee, and possibly the use of a car to attend an occasional movie. The school found a bike for me, and a student who had a car at the school volunteered to provide transportation to a movie location in Hughesville, a tiny community just a short distance from Charlotte Hall. The movie was shown in what looked like a store front with a big bay window, and the film was projected onto a wall or portable screen. Folding chairs were used for seating the 8-10 people in the small room. If we called to ask for the movie's starting time in Hughesville, the answer was "When can you arrive?" and that's no joke.

Weekends on my College campus

My four years as a student at Western Maryland College (WMC) covered 1948-1952, and I had no access to a car during those years. I can honestly say that I never thought I was handicapped by the absence of a car. In those years, the WMC enrollment was perhaps 700-800 students, and most students resided in campus dormitories and most ate their meals in the college dining hall. I was one resident of that population. Other students, those living and eating off campus, were called "Day Hops," and they were few in number. WMC students typically carried a full academic load of about 14-18 class hours per week, and nearly all classes met on a Monday thru Friday sequence. As for the weekends, on-campus social or athletic events were scheduled for about one weekend in four, and the other two or three weekends were termed "quiet weekends." Resident students frequently left (fled) the campus on those weekends, either to avoid boredom or perhaps desiring to have parents at home wash their soiled clothes. I loved the WMC quiet weekends, so I became a weekend fixture on campus, seldom journeying the thirty miles to my home in Frederick, Maryland.

I recall that weekends, and especially Sundays, were always enjoyable days for me on the WMC campus. Those days played a vital role in my busy seven-day schedule. Unlike other resident students who viewed weekends and Sundays as "do nothing days," I wanted and needed that free time to catch up on back academic assignments and to work ahead on long-term projects. My personal college goal was to maintain at least a "B" academic average and to receive "A" grades in Mathematics, my major field of study. I had no desire to slight the non-academic aspects of WMC life solely for the sake of a higher grade average, thus choosing not to compete with Pre-Med majors and other students who did seek straight "A" averages. I could be counted on to work all weekend meals as a student waiter, and I sincerely believed that those away from campus over weekends were missing the best meals of the week.

Rotarian Gallagher does not own a car

Gus Gallagher and his wife, Rita, live in Washington, DC, and they contend that owning a family car is not a consideration for them. Gus and I were constantly kidding each other on a variety of topics, but no kidding was involved when he ruled out car ownership as a part of his life. He and Rita travel all over the world, and they are constantly on the go, but I often heard them remark: "Why would we want to own a car, living in Washington, DC, as we do?" I can appreciate their thinking on the matter. Gus and Rita never miss a Rotary International Convention, and when I am able to attend these annual June meetings of Rotary, Gus and Rita usually invite me to join their many other friends to a birthday party for Gus. It is not uncommon to see the highest officials of Rotary International at these popular affairs. Gus and Rita are charming hosts.

TWO RETIRED POLICE CARS EXPANDED MY WORLD:

My first purchase of a car

My senior year as a student at Western Maryland College began in September of 1951 and ended in May of 1952. It was an enjoyable time for me, as were the other three years, but it was a hectic year as well. Taking exams and making future plans required a lot of thought and decision-making. One decision I made was to buy my first car. A two-year fellowship for graduate study would take me in the fall of 1952 to Wesleyan University in Middletown, Connecticut, and that undertaking would require a car for transportation. Also, I had a summer job offer as a timekeeper for the Thomas Canning Company in Gaithersburg, MD, provided I had access to a car. Dad suggested that I buy a retired police car, and he felt he could arrange for me to acquire the car that had been used by the Frederick City Chief of Police. It would have low mileage, and it would be in excellent condition. That car was obtained, but one drawback was that it looked like an inverted bathtub. To make matters worse, Dad painted the wheels red, and it then took on the appearance of a farm wagon. One other problem was that occasionally the gears on the Ford would lock. When that happened, you had to jump out of the car and rock it until the gears snapped back into place. Picture my embarrassment when such a car problem actually occurred in the middle of a busy intersection in Quebec.

Summer employment was a necessity

For as long as I can remember, the summers of my youth were always times for me to hold a variety of jobs, jobs that paid money rather than jobs that only offered an appreciative pat on the head. My family lived in Frederick, Maryland, in the 1930s and 1940s, and money was always a scarce commodity. In those years, my father was the sole breadwinner for the family, and he did his best with a limited amount of schooling. Like many boys in farm families in the 1920s, he did not complete high school. Dad's abilities qualified him as a jack-of-all-trades, but he is best remembered as a Frederick City policeman and as a fine automobile mechanic. In sharp contrast, my mother was well-educated, holding a degree from Hood College, but she never actively sought full-time employment outside the home. Mom was a great cook, so we never lacked for tasty meals, and she also enjoyed sewing. I recall that I often wore shirts to school that she made from feed sacks, and my corduroy pants were adjusted hand-me-downs from my older brother. (Those pants never seemed to wear out!) I would not classify our Shook family as a poverty case, but it was clearly understood that my outside jobs would be the source of most of my spending money, and I often had three jobs at the same time.

Between 1948 and 1952, my under-graduate college years were spent at Western Maryland College (WMC) located in Westminster, MD. Western Maryland was a Methodist affiliated college, and as a consequence, many Methodist families sent their children to WMC. Another characteristic of the College was its reasonable cost, a cost that was relatively low compared to costs of other private colleges. For this reason, WMC entering students generally came from middle-income and lower-income families, and most were residents of Maryland. Some fortunate students gained State of Maryland scholarships that covered nearly all costs at WMC, and for others, the College had a few endowed grants to assist needy students. One such $200-300 WMC grant was awarded only for the freshman year, and in subsequent years, the student was required to hold a campus job to earn the equivalent funds.

In my final three years at WMC, my job was that of a dining hall waiter, a job also held by 30-40 other students. For a small percentage of my college classmates, the summer break from studies could be viewed as a time for recreation, relaxation, and possibly for world travel, but for the rest of us, summer jobs were essential as a source of money to meet college and living expenses. Those holding campus jobs during the college year would certainly have needed summer jobs. The summer break from college lasted at least two months, and many of my WMC classmates chose to work during those summer months at a beach resort such as that located in Ocean City, MD. Some needy students could not hold campus jobs for fear that grades would suffer, and for those students, summer jobs were an even more critical money source.

Pearly Dukes and the migratory workers

Along with the income, I found that most summer employment provided valuable learning experiences that were not available in college classrooms. A good example of this would be my summer employment in 1952 and 1953. The job I held in those summers was that of "timekeeper" for the Thomas Canning Company in Gaithersburg, Maryland. Thanks to that employment, I was introduced to Pearly Dukes and his group of migratory workers from Alabama. A canning factory was the setting for the work experience, and the work would prove to be both unique and memorable. Some of my past summer jobs had included picking apples at McCain's Orchard in Frederick, driving a wobbly-wheel on road construction

21

projects, pressing clothes on a steam press, bagging cracker meal and dog food at a bakery, carpentry work in home construction, part-time mail delivery, etc. All of those temporary jobs brought me income and associations that I would not have had otherwise, but none proved as valuable to me as did my contact with Pearly Dukes and his migratory workers.

The time keeper role was a new challenge for me, requiring that I complete all employment documents, record the hours worked by each worker, calculate all salaries, issue weekly pay envelopes, and tabulate tax forms for each employee. Since workers often ate meals at the factory (I hesitate to call the eating area a "dining hall"), I also needed to adjust pay slips to show deductions for the cost of meals consumed by each worker. There were no housing charges to deduct, because the only housing units at the factory were sheds with no heat, and old mattresses were placed on the floors to serve as bedding. Some of the sheds had no doors, and migratory workers, male and female, had little opportunity for privacy. In Gaithersburg, in the early 1950s, the migratory workers were all black, and some workers arrived with babies in their arms, violating the rules established by the canning factory.

The Thomas Canning Factory had arranged for Pearly Dukes to deliver the group of migratory workers, and all in the group had made the long trip from Tuskegee, Alabama, packed into the back of a worn out, open-back truck. Pearly knew that the truck he drove was unsafe and that his journey with unprotected passengers violated many existing traffic laws. For this reason, my first impression of Mr. Dukes was not a favorable one. It became obvious to me that Pearly Dukes had no difficulty in assembling Tuskegee men and women and children to join him on his annual trip to Gaithersburg. Pearly knew that many unemployed people would jump at the chance to gain work, even though the pay was low and travel conditions were harsh. Most upsetting to me was the fact that Dukes not only charged the workers for their transportation in his truck, but he also expected a cut from each worker's weekly salary. Workers received weekly payments in cash on Saturday mornings, and Pearly was always standing at the door to receive his share from each pay envelope. In addition, the canning factory agreed to pay Dukes an hourly wage, as though he occupied a position on the production line, which he did not. It upset me that he provided no visible leadership or support for members of the migratory group. It gave me no pleasure to place a pay envelope in the hand of Pearly Dukes each Saturday, and I possessed no warm feelings for this memorable character.

It was hard for me to fully understand why the migratory workers showed affection for Pearly Dukes. They did not seem to resent giving him money from each of their weekly-pay envelopes, and they willingly paid his charge for transportation in an open-back truck. Their thinking seemed to be that working at the canning factory in Gaithersburg, Maryland, was better than life would have been back in Tuskegee, and that Dukes was the person who made this opportunity possible. At least in Maryland, jobs were available, and the workers did receive a small amount of money to spend each week. The money I placed in their pay envelopes each Saturday morning was usually gone within two hours, and what remained, after giving Pearly Dukes his share of the money, was taken to the store across the street from the factory. The workers returned from the store carrying their purchases of candy and trinkets. There was no money remaining to be saved, and there was no money to be mailed to relatives back home in Tuskegee.

The members of the migratory group were not carefully screened by Pearly Dukes prior to departing Tuskegee, and this created major problems for me as the timekeeper for the canning factory in Gaithersburg, Maryland. Many of those arriving in the back of the truck driven from Alabama did not know their ages, their dates of birth, or even the names of their parents. Employment laws required that workers at the canning factory be of a certain age, and all workers needed to possess a valid Social Security Number. Only after a great effort on my part were most of the group members eventually qualified to work in the canning factory. Nevertheless, a few were rejected and left to survive on their own. On the positive side, I did find that these migratory workers were generally hard workers and not prone to be lazy as some seemed to expect. To no one's surprise, their educational levels were typically low, but most migratory workers could offer satisfactory performances when engaging in the required canning factory tasks. I learned to like the members of the migratory group, but Pearly Dukes did little to gain my affection. In my opinion, he took unfair advantage of the workers in his group, and I compared him to a pimp controlling a group of women who are often forced to sell themselves on the city streets.

My summer timekeeper role in the early 1950s was a worthwhile learning experience, and I felt that my pay was adequate. As timekeeper, my hourly wage was only $.95, which sounds small, but my total hours worked each week tended to be large. Some weeks, my work hours actually approached 100, and it was not unusual for me to work, sleep and eat at the factory for six straight days, commuting to my home in Frederick only on Sundays. If my memory is correct, the migratory workers during that time must have received no more than $.65 or $.70 an hour for their work, if that much. I gained a great respect for migratory workers in those summers, and I recognized the valuable service that these workers provide annually to the US economy. On the negative side, I also witnessed the harsh treatment that these workers had to endure as they migrated from work place to work place. In my opinion, the Gaithersburg factory and other employers of migratory workers had to eliminate these harsh conditions, especially practices such as the use of open-back trucks for transporting workers and the lack of suitable housing and adequate medical care. My summer job in those two years was a valuable experience, an experience not readily available in any college classroom.

Wesleyan University vacation breaks

My first car, the Ford that resembled an inverted bathtub, transported me safely between my home in Maryland to Wesleyan University in Middletown, Connecticut, and this lengthy trip occurred some five or six times over my two years of graduate study at Wesleyan. For most of 1952-1954, the car remained in a college parking lot, because I seldom had need of it. I could walk to the classroom buildings, and the fraternity house providing my meals was just a few blocks from my residence in the Weeks House. The Weeks House was owned by the University, and served as headquarters of my graduate program. It had been a former home for a Connecticut governor named Weeks, and I truly loved the luxury it provided me. I was one of twelve students admitted to the first class of the University's new Masters of Arts in Teaching program started in 1952, and twelve new graduate students were to be added each year that followed. Each of the twenty-four MAT students would enter with a two-year fellowship which covered all costs of the education, namely tuition and room & board expenses. My interest in singing attracted me to membership in the University Choir and I also was soloist for the local Middletown Methodist Church, located on the edge of the campus. Wesleyan was all male in the 1950s, so our choir was often joined for major concerts by the girls of the Radcliffe College choir.

One of my MAT buddies was Joe Colannino from Brooklyn, NY, and my seldom used car transported us to visit his home over a Wesleyan University's vacation break. Joe had never been to the Statue of Liberty or up in the Empire State Building, but after my stay, he could no longer claim that to be true. We attended a game at Ebbets Field, home of the Brooklyn Dodgers. This Major

League Baseball park was located in the Flatbush section of Brooklyn. On this visit to Joe's home his family proved to me that a Sunday meal could last for four hours. Another member of the 1952 entering MAT class was a French major named John Frantzis, and he and I journeyed to Canada for one of the other vacation breaks from graduate school studies. While touring Quebec, my Ford decided it was a good time to lock its gears, so the car came to a halt in the middle of a busy intersection. John Francis followed my lead as we jumped out of the car and began rocking it, forward and backward. Soon a loud click could be heard, and we were then able to drive away from the intersection and the growing number of curious onlookers. The lunch served to us at the famous Chateau Frontenac was another memorable moment of that day in Quebec, memorable because I had a delicious meal while my French major friend did not. The waitress kindly spoke English to take my order, noticing my difficulty with the menu, but she spoke Quebec French with John because he resisted the use of English. The problem was that John's French was nothing like Quebec French, and he ended up with very little to eat. Only one of us recognized the humor in the event, and it was hard for me to suppress my laughter. Poor John!

"The Rose City" welcomed me in 1954

I believe that it was in 1956 that the Chief of Police of Frederick City, MD, once again traded in his Ford vehicle for a new one, and as the old saying goes "I was Johnny on the spot." My father was still a member of the Frederick police force, and that could have been a factor in my getting the low mileage car. The police car I obtained in 1952 had served me well, but I was happy to replace it with a much more attractive model, one that did not resemble an inverted bathtub. I should also point out that my new "used car" no longer had a siren or red light on the roof, and I doubt if it could have exceeded 85 mph, but I gave it no such test. This car would serve me well for the next six years, during which time I would hold three different occupations.

In 1954, while I still owned the first of my two police cars, a phone call from the Superintendent of Schools of Madison, NJ, invited me to visit his town and become a part of the Madison High School faculty. I loved everything about this small city, and I would be teaching Geometry and Algebra in a highly-rated academic school. A two-year military service obligation was hanging over my head, but the school saw that as no problem. Ward Shoemaker, Principal of Madison High, said that I was a perfect fit, and I signed the $3,550 contract shown on the next page. Principal Shoemaker was a person I grew to love and admire, and he was the friend for me to consult whenever tough decisions needed to be made.

In anyone's lifetime, there are critical moments when important decisions need to be made, and at those times, a close personal friend may be needed to offer a sympathetic ear. For me, Principal Ward Shoemaker of Madison High was such a person. After my second year of teaching in Madison, New Jersey, a decision had to be made about a new job offer that would return me to work for my undergraduate college, Western Maryland College. I knew that Ward would help me to think through the complex issues to arrive at the proper decision outcome. Because of his special qualities, I knew that his advice would be sound, and he would never allow his role as Madison High's Principal to bias the conversation. He and I sat in his back yard of his Madison home to hold the discussion, and I realized how lucky I was to have Ward Shoemaker as a close friend.

Form A-22 100M 11-19-52

EMPLOYMENT CONTRACT

It is agreed between the Board of Education of __the Borough of Madison__
in the County of __Morris__ party of the first part, and __H. Kenneth Shook__ party
of the second part, that said Board of Education has employed and does hereby engage and employ the
said party of the second part to __teach__ in the public schools, under the control of said
Board of Education, from the __1st__ day of __September__, 19 __54__, to the __30th__
day of __June__, 19 __55__, at the salary of $ __3,550.00__ to be paid in
__20__ equal * __semi-monthly__ installments: _____

_____ that the said party of the second part shall begin service on the_____
day of_____, 19____, that the said party of the second part holds an appropriate
_____certificate issued in New Jersey now in full force and effect, or will procure
such certificate before the date said person shall begin service and that the date when said certificate
will expire is the_____day of_____, 19____, and that said person, before enter-
ing upon the duties of such position, will exhibit the certificate to the County Superintendent of Schools
and to the Superintendent of the district in which such school is situate, or to the Secretary or District
Clerk in districts where there is no Superintendent.

The said party of the second part hereby accepts the employment aforesaid and agrees to faith-
fully do and perform duties under the employment aforesaid, and to observe and enforce the rules
prescribed for the government of the school by the Board of Education.

It is hereby agreed by the parties hereto that this contract may at any time be terminated by either
party giving to the other __sixty__ days' notice in writing of intention to terminate the same, but
that in the absence of any provision herein for a definite number of days' notice, the contract shall run
for the full term named above.

Dated this __13th__ day of __May__, 19 __54__, Board of Education of

the __Borough__ of __Madison__ in the
(Town or City)   (Name of District)

County of __Morris__
(County)

President _____

Employee _____

Attest _____ District Clerk or Secretary

* Insert monthly or semi-monthly.

Notes—This is a specimen contract that should be modified in accordance with the terms of employment.

R.S. 18:13-7—"In every contract, unless otherwise specified, a month shall be construed and taken to be
twenty school days or four weeks of five school days each. The salary specified in every contract shall be paid in
equal semi-monthly or monthly installments, as the Board of Education shall determine, not later than five days
after the first and fifteenth days of each month in the case of semi-monthly installments and not later than
five days after the close of each month in the case of monthly installments while the school is in session."

Ed Holl   Principal Ward Shoemaker

Ed Holl hand-sketched Christmas cards

Phyllis Fredericks, Ed Holl, and I became the three additions to the faculty of Madison High in September of 1954. Phyllis brought her beauty to the English Department, and Ed brought his talent and energy to the Art Department. In that year, it was my good fortune to share an art classroom with Ed, and he became my closest friend. He placed the geometric designs of my students on display in the hallways of the school. Over the years, Ed made hand-sketched Christmas cards for close friends, and, with his wife's approval, I show some of his sketches on these pages. It is sad to report that Ed passed away in his early retirement years.

During my two years of teaching at Madison High school, I was fortunate to acquire a room in the home of Mrs. Sharp. She lived just two doors away from the school, and she was a Methodist minister's widow. She allowed me the use of her one-car garage and also her refrigerator. In return, I often drove her to the Methodist Church on Sundays and helped her to visit shopping centers. My singing ability quickly gained me an invitation to become part of the Methodist Church choir, and I became their tenor soloist. The choir director also arranged for me to sing in musical productions at Centenary College, located in nearby Hackettstown, New Jersey. I recall driving the icy roads to attend rehearsals at Centenary, and in one show, I enjoyed singing the very popular tune *Lady Be Good to Me*.

Fort Monmouth welcomed me in 1955

It was in 1955 that I began my two-year military obligation, and my "basic training" in South Carolina proved to be a rather unique experience. The trainers saw that I had completed a four-year ROTC program in college, and they did not know what to do with me. Had my right leg not received a football injury, I would have been given a rank of Second Lieutenant. Skipping most of "basic training," I moved on to Fort Monmouth, New Jersey, for the remainder of my two-year service obligation. What I encountered there was far from what I expected. Basic training does a good job in the sense that trainees are prepared to follow orders without question, and the accepted goal is combat readiness. Those of us selected to enter R&D (Research & Development) Company were all scientists and mathematicians with college graduate degrees. We were in the military, but we were also expected to work in computer labs under civilian bosses. These labs were not on the base, and some men of R&D

Company would drive their own cars to the labs, and some men would ride in a military bus to and from the labs.

A diagram I once used in presentations identified the two groups that make up R&D Company. Group A referred to the "men" who worked in the labs when not doing military duties, and Group B, comprised the "officers and staff" who remained on base and ran the daily activities of R&D Company. The diagram also indicated the transactions between the two groups, interactions often found to be points of friction and conflict. Group A felt that lab work was their primary reason for being assigned to R&D Company, and Group B was just as determined to make R&D Company a combat-ready military unit, work in the labs being a secondary goal. The greatest conflict seemed to exist when the company officers were career military persons who had not attended a college or university. Officers who obtained their rank through a college ROTC type of program seemed to have fewer problems with their R&D Company command. Civilian bosses at the labs wanted the men of Group A to work on a schedule approaching full-time, but they seldom entered the disputes that existed between Group A and Group B.

On the very first day I arrived at R&D Company, following my weeks of basic training, I needed to march with the company members in a Company Review parade. Company officers wanted R&D Company to make a nice showing in comparison to other companies on the base, but that would not happen. As we approached the parade area, persons in the back of the company formation came filtering up between ranks, making the formation double its normal width and blocking all traffic. After adjusting the formation, the officers positioned our group with the other company groups and we approached the reviewing stand. Imagine how shocked I was to observe others in the formation swinging their arms in a manner opposite to a normal swing. Also, some marchers in our group had lowered their helmet liners to the point that eyes were hidden. The audience watching the parade found R&D Company to be great fun, and they applauded enthusiastically. Our R&D Company officers did not react in a similar fashion. In the days that followed, we were given extra military duties and extra drill practice, and seldom did we have time for our laboratory work. Clearly, the actions taken by Group A and by Group B were often correctly viewed as gestures intended to antagonize the other side, and acts of retaliation were sure to follow.

On one occasion, which I now relate, the officer group miscalculated the intent of an action on the part of one individual. A soldier with a bad case of sun glare wore his sunglasses in a parade. The officers announced that no such glasses would be allowed in the next parade. On the day of the next parade, I would estimate that at least fifteen persons were wearing sunglasses, and they produced medical slips to justify their use of sunglasses at all outdoor functions. The R&D Company officers could not overrule the authority of the medical slips. In a second example, I had placed a large piece of plywood under the mattress of my barrack's cot, and I explained that my bad back seemed to require it for a restful night's sleep. The board would have been removed had I not obtained a medical slip from the Post Medical Officer to allow me the use of the board. In my older years, the same back condition requires me to use a firm mattress but no board.

Surprise barrack inspections and extra KP duties were often employed by Group B officers to demonstrate control over the men of Group A. No provocation by Group A was needed to motivate these actions, but on two occasions, a provocative action by Group A did exist. On one day at the labs, we were all called back to our company area, and we were forced to go through the mess hall line to be served food a second time on the same morning. It seems that many of the men were wasting food, and the officers were forcing the men to eat properly. The officer's desired goal was not attained by this action of recalling the men from the computer labs. On another occasion, the men of R&D Company intentionally made poor showings on physical fitness tests, and most did not meet the minimum requirements. All were forced to repeat the tests, and the results did not change. At this point, the officers in charge found a simpler solution to the problem. The scores were elevated to the level that all members of R&D Company passed the fitness tests.

Reflecting back, decades later, there are a variety of possible solutions to the problems faced by any similar R&D Company in the military. The nature of the solutions depends on the slant of the observer, as favoring one of the two groups that made up such a company or seeking a more middle-ground position on the issues. In my opinion, one thing is certain. A clear directive is needed from an authority higher than the company level, stating the goals for such a company. The "officers" and the "men" of such a company should not be placed in the roles of combatants, forcing one side to seek its goal of "military preparedness" while the other would strive for a different goal, that of "significant achievement in the laboratory." Perhaps in times of peace, when the country is not at war, the latter goal can be allowed to prevail. The attached photo of me wearing a gas mask is inserted here to prove that I did spend some time away from the labs.

The linkage of two turnpikes

The two turnpikes that most often impacted on my travel by automobile were and are the Pennsylvania and New Jersey turnpikes. For the life of my first car, 1952-1955, I traveled north on the Jersey turnpike to reach Wesleyan University in Connecticut and north to reach Madison High School in Madison, New Jersey. Returning to my home in Frederick, Maryland, I usually traveled south on the Jersey turnpike.

A memorable experience occurred in 1956 after I purchased my second car, another retired police car. On this particular trip from Fort Monmouth, NJ, to Frederick, MD, I was traveling south on the Jersey turnpike, and I was fighting sleep. The car radio was loud and the car windows were wide open to provide a constant air flow. I drove on the right edge of the three- or four-lane highway, and I focused only on the white line to my right side. When I became suddenly aware of crossing over a bridge and approaching a toll booth, I also became wide awake. The only bridge and toll booth I could remember was at the end of the turnpike. Was it possible that I passed the toll booth at the south end of the Jersey turnpike without knowing it? Did I crash through a toll gate? Arriving at a toll gate, I paid a toll and asked the attendant where I was. He said that I just entered the Pennsylvania turnpike. The new connection to the Jersey turnpike had just opened in May of 1956, unknown to me. It may have been a laughing matter, but it also convinced me that a nap at the toll booth location would be needed before continuing my journey home.

Autos in the middle years (1960-1989)

College employment and early years of marriage:

The new Dodge was a wedding gift

When Carol Jennette accepted my proposal of marriage, a June 1960 wedding was planned, and the event would take place in the large Baker Chapel, located on the Western Maryland College campus. The President of the College, Dr. Lowell Ensor, would assist in the service, and I believe his daughter's wedding was the only wedding that preceded my wedding in the new Baker Chapel. Carol's father was a prominent physician in Carroll County, and the friends of the Jennette family would easily fill half of the Baker Chapel. My parents and our Shook family relatives mainly lived in Frederick County, some 30 miles distant, and help would be needed to fill the second side of the large Chapel. Fortunately, my employment at the College and my numerous Westminster community activities allowed me to develop many friendships, and those persons arriving late for the service would move to the side with the most open seats.

The reception that followed the service was held at the Jennette home, and the beautiful June weather allowed the reception to take place out of doors. It was truly a festive occasion. The reception seemed to last for hours, but Carol and I finally made our escape, as shown below. We

departed from the front door of the house with rice in our hair and smiles on our faces. Carol and I then discovered that our chariot would be a new Dodge Dart, thanks to the generosity of Carol's parents. The Dodge Dart was white in color, and it now came with streamers, and numerous tin cans were attached to the rear of the car. Other photos show

the happy couple enjoying a week in Bermuda, and the final picture shows the new husband unloading the Dodge Dart after a pleasant honeymoon. The car was parked on Green Street, near our new second-floor Westminster apartment.

Dr. Jennette's Chrysler Imperial

When Dr. Jennette gave us a Dodge Dart as a wedding gift, I believe he sought our advice as to which car we preferred, but his other car purchases seemed to follow a different pattern. Apparently he alone picked out a car in secret, and then entered a show room unannounced and made an offer for a specific car. Essentially he said, "Here is my offer. Take it or leave it." He never wanted to negotiate a price, and some dealers learned this lesson too late, as they watched Dr. Jennette depart the showroom. In the early-1960s, the Jennette family car was a Chrysler Imperial, and Carol and I often rode with Carol's parents on the Sundays of Baltimore Colt home football games. We would stop for lunch at the Green Spring Inn before driving on to the stadium on 33rd Street in Baltimore. Dr. Jennette served the Baltimore Colts as their medical doctor during the training camps held in Westminster, and annually, he was assigned a stadium parking space and given upper-deck tickets for all home games. Carol and I usually sat in the upper-deck seats, while her parents preferred to sit in end zone seats, seats protected from possible rain or snow.

Speaking of snow, Dr. Jennette often joked that on bad snow days, he suspected that some Carroll County residents sought medical aid at their farm houses only because his car would help open their clogged country lanes. The car best suited for his trips in the heavy snow was said to have been a Plymouth with high wheels, a car like those used by persons delivering mail. Dr. Jennette also laughed when he read a newspaper report of an accident that had taken place while returning to Westminster from his Baltimore hospital calls. In the article, it said that he was accompanied in his car by some woman who claimed to be his wife. Mrs. Jennette was quick to assure us that she was, in fact, the woman in his car that day.

We were a one-car family in 1960

Carol and I started our married life with one family car, the Dodge Dart. These were early years in the 1960's, and it was not an unusual condition in this time period for a husband and wife to share the use of one family car. This was especially true for newly married couples. If both partners in the marriage were employed outside the home, sharing one car took much thought and careful family planning. The trend toward more women in the workplace was an established fact of the 1950's and the 1960's, but mothers with young children still tended to favor a stay-at-home role if at all possible.

My employment as a college admissions officer required frequent travel to secondary schools in a six-state area, and some travel forced me to be away from home for three or four successive days. A college car was generally made available for my use. On these occasions, my wife could have full use of the family car, provided I had a way to get to the campus to pick up the college car. My admissions travel was especially heavy during the months of September, October, and November, and a dedicated effort on my part could yield a successful recruitment year. My young son often gave me a send-off as I departed from home. One morning, he reminded me of the possible negative impact of business travel on the family when he said, "Daddy, thank you for coming." It was hard for me to focus on my school visits that day.

In a lighter and more humorous vein, I can still recall an occasion when I employed my trusted logic to solve a minor transportation problem. On that particular day, I was interviewing student applicants on campus in the morning, and the late afternoon schedule was unusually light. I decided to leave work early and walk the short distance to my home. The weather was pleasant for walking, and I saw no reason for my wife to drive our car to the campus to pick me up.

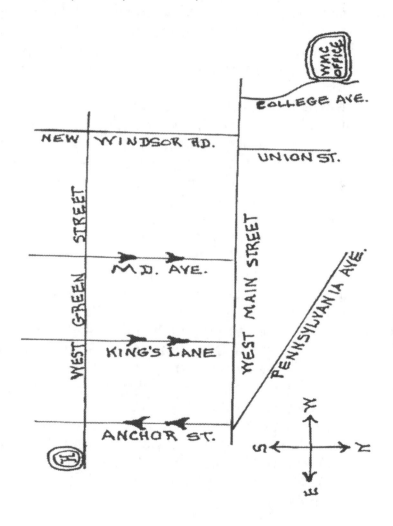

Rather than phone my wife (the easy way out), I quickly sketched the map shown above and the logic began to flow. My use of superior logic determined the route I would walk from the college to my home. If I reasoned correctly, I would select the exact path my wife would drive, if she drove to the campus to pick me up. In that way, I could intercept her before she arrived at my office. In the sketch, the College is located upper right, and my home is located at the lower left. West Green and West Main ran east and west, and an alley ran parallel between these two streets. I did not diagram the alley, because my wife would not select an alley for her drive to the campus. The three one-way streets also added to the complexity and fun of the logic problem.

The one-way streets did reduce the options open to my wife (she seldom drove the wrong way on a one-way street). If you have looked at the sketch, you correctly concluded that there were three choices for my wife to consider. She had to use Green and Main streets, but she could select King's Lane or Maryland Avenue or New Windsor Road to connect the two streets. I decided that New Windsor Road would be the choice, and that was the route I walked from campus to my home. I felt confident of my decision as I walked home that afternoon, and at no time did my wife drive past me heading in the opposite direction toward the college campus. My wife was, in fact, at home when I completed my pleasant walk, but my car was not there. The car was back at the college. It seems that I had driven the family car to work that morning. Quietly, without Carol knowing, I slipped out the back door of the house and quickly covered the distance to the campus to retrieve the family car. My logic was not at fault that day, but the original premise was incorrect. My wife had not kept the car that day! I had. [Note: When writing your memoirs, be sure that you make fun of yourself and not someone else.]

"Admissions" travel in College cars

As stated in a prior memoir, my role as head of the admissions operation of Western Maryland College necessitated that I visit high schools and college fairs, and these visits took me mainly to meetings in Maryland, Pennsylvania, New Jersey, Delaware, Virginia, West Virginia, and the District of Columbia. Concentric circles drawn around the College's location in Westminster, MD, made it clear that most applicants preferred to attend a college that was no more than two or three hours' drive from their home. In 1958-1960, I worked alone, except for a part-time secretary, and I annually visited nearly 150 secondary schools. In later years, when additional assistants could be hired, we made annual visits to about 275 of our best feeder schools. No one at the College had a higher priority for the use of college cars than did our Admissions Office recruiters, so our needs were always met. This arrangement was especially important during the heavy travel months of September, October, November and December. All admissions recruiters of the various colleges have stories to tell about visits that went bad, and I also recall occasions when I learned by my mistakes in judgment.

Here I list a few travel plans that turned out other than the way that they were originally planned. One lesson I quickly learned was that if you plan to visit schools the following morning on the east side of the Delaware Memorial Bridge, it make little sense to spend the prior night in a motel that is located on the west side of the bridge? The only time I made such a decision, heavy fog caused a major accident on the bridge early the next morning, and I was forced to reschedule two of my school visits planned for the next day. Or, thinking of another occasion, does it make sense to ever take off for northern New Jersey without first making a reservation for that night's lodging? Well, to my surprise, on this particular cold November date, the few motels in the rural area of NJ were all filled, and I actually spent that uncomfortable night trying to sleep in the cold car. About every hour, I started the engine, and the car's heater worked its magic to warm the interior of the car and its one occupant. It was a night I'll not forget.

And, yet, another example of poor planning was when I parked the college car in the circular entrance to a Howard County school in Maryland, parking just long enough to unload admissions material and a slide projector. The counselor rushed out to help me and said that our time for a session had been cut short. "Just leave the car where it is!" she said. I did as she instructed, but I forgot that the car's keys were still in the ignition. After the brief session with students I found that the car was still parked in the driveway but the keys were gone from the car. My great logic reasoned that someone had turned the keys into the main office, and they had, but then the keys had been given to another visitor who happened to be in the building at precisely the same time. That person left the school with my keys and was finally tracked down having coffee in a local restaurant. The delay caused me to miss my second school visit that day, and I left a note for the employee of Western Maryland College who was already in route to the Howard County secondary school, bringing me a second set of car keys. This story is just another example of how not to start the work day.

S&H Green Stamps and Hanover visits

In my many travels, both in a college supplied vehicle and in the family car, S&H Green Stamps were often received when we purchased gasoline. Especially in the 1960s, Carol and I accumulated numerous books of stamps, and the nearest store to redeem the books for prizes was a store located in Hanover, PA. I honestly do not recall any of the items we acquired in that decade, but the visits to Hanover are vivid in my memory.

When visiting Hanover in the 1960s, we often attended the movie theater there, and, when time allowed, another favorite destination of ours was the Conowingo Dairy.

Our choice of an ice cream treat at that store was called a Pig's Dinner, and it was served in a wooden trough with at least three dips of ice cream. Another offering was called a Battleship, and if the first was eaten in the store by one person, the second Battleship was free. We never purchased this monster serving and never saw anyone else receive a second serving. A Hanover store, just a few blocks away from the theater and dairy, was the one that sold us our bedroom furniture when Carol and I were married in 1960. More than 50 years later, many residents of Westminster, MD, still enjoy visits to Hanover, PA, to do their shopping and dining.

Some family cars were station wagons

The Pontiac dealership in Westminster, MD, sold (or rented) driver-trainer cars to the Carroll County high schools, and if those vehicles were not abused by student drivers, citizens could acquire a slightly used car at a reduced price.

In 1963, it was hard to believe that a huge Pontiac station wagon was among this lot of cars, and the low mileage on the vehicle convinced us we had a bargain too good to pass up. It would be great to have such a vehicle for the annual trips our family took to Ocean City, MD. Pictured above is a photo taken in the early-1970s, and it shows my wife and children with their rental bikes, and the Ocean City boardwalk can be seen in the background on a bright sunny day.

The woman driver screamed, "Pig! Pig!"

The picture of the Ocean City boardwalk shown above reminds me of another event in my life that also took place in Ocean City, MD. I believe the month would have been October or November. You are correct if you assume that Ocean City is the popular vacation spot for most visitors during June, July, and August, but I prefer to visit at a less crowded time of year. My logic concludes that October is a great time to avoid crowds in Ocean City, and the costs for housing and meals are much more reasonable than in the summer months. Also, I enjoy riding a bike on the boardwalk, and the restrictions on such an activity are mainly lifted in the off-months.

This particular visit to Ocean City did not include the entire family, and I transported my one workable bike from Westminster, MD, on the back of our family car. My wife has reminded me on numerous occasions that my efforts to save money on bike rentals has been offset by the scratches made by the bike rack on the car's trunk lid. Nevertheless, on this sunny day in Ocean City the bike was proving its worth, as Carol and I alternated the use of the bike every half-hour. In thirty minutes, each of us could make three round trips of the total boardwalk. At one end of the boardwalk was the Dunes Manor Hotel where we often enjoyed evening meals, and prices were reduced if the meal was ordered prior to 6:00 pm. Heading north on the boardwalk, the wind usually met us head on, making it a bit more difficult to pedal, but heading south, the wind pushed us along at a comfortable speed. At the south end of the ride was a large display case containing a very large fish. I thought it was a shark or sword fish, but Carol insists it is a marlin. Whatever!

While standing by my bike and observing the fish on display, a female voice behind me exclaimed "Thank heavens, it was caught by a woman!" I was laughing as I turned to see the source of the remark. What I saw was a bicycle built for four, and it contained a mother and her two children. The mother was quite attractive, and her children were 6-8 in ages. The children occupied the front seat, and they had pedals to assist the mother in propelling the bike. We introduced ourselves, and I thanked Sandy for designating who caught the huge fish.

Still looking at the bicycle that was built to resemble a carriage, I was tempted to begin singing the old song "Daisy Bell," of course, changing the final line of the chorus to: "But you'd look sweet upon the seat of a bicycle built for (two) <u>four</u>." A smile came to my face as I recalled that Dacre, the English composer, brought his bike to the United States, paying a duty, and someone remarked his duty would have doubled had he brought a "bicycle built for two." After hearing the remark, he added the phrase to his song, and the rest is history.

As we headed our bikes north on the Ocean City boardwalk, I offered to share a "woman driver joke," and before Sandy could refuse my offer, I told the following: Two men were joy-riding in their convertible and the car was racing up a long hill. They had just voted unanimously that women were the cause of most auto accidents when a car came over the hill ahead of them darting from their side of the road to the other. As if to prove the conclusion the men had just reached, the other car was driven by a woman. They yelled at her "Woman driver!" She screamed back, "Pig! Pig!" The angry men continued over the hill and wrecked their car trying to avoid a pig that had somehow wandered on to the country road. My Ocean City listeners found the joke to their liking.

The woman on the other bike was Sandy Pagnotti, a successful business executive and the wife of a well-known Baltimore television personality. Her two daughters were Alee and Annie. Their enjoyment of my joke was soon to be revealed. I passed them three more times on this bike ride, and each time that we came near to each other, the girls called out the loud warning, "Pig! Pig!" The greatest praise a joke teller can receive is to hear his punch line repeated by appreciative listeners. Sandy Pagnotti and her daughters may not have caught a record-size fish worthy of public display, but on their 1999 visit to Ocean City, MD, the three Pagnotti girls did warm the heart of this writer of memoirs.

Family reunions and a Florida trip

In the photograph shown above, John and I are in front, and Carol, Bill and Jennette are in the rear. We looked this way in the early 1970s. All family members had a love for sports and music, and Carol was kept busy transporting the children to their various activities. Other than trips to Ocean City, MD, in the summers, most family travel was limited to a few local destinations. Two exceptions do come to mind. We did attend family reunions which were held annually on a relative's farm, and there was the one family trip to Orlando, Florida, in 1972.Below is a typical reunion group photo, and my wife and I are in the back right. I was the photographer at most of our reunions, so this was a nice change for me, actually being in front of the camera and not behind it. I credit the good camera work to Richard Burgee, a cousin who lost his life to cancer in recent years.

Most of the family members attending our annual reunions had Burgee as their last name, and to explain my attendance, my mother's maiden name was Burgee. The Shook family greatly enjoyed these events called "Burgee Reunions," and we never felt out of place. In the 1970s and 1980s, reunions were possibly held at amusement parks or public parks near Frederick, MD, but by the 1990s, our group met at what was then called the Burgee's Home Farm, located near Betty's Green Valley Animal Hospital. A June 14, 1998, reunion program bulletin included such words and phrases as: "37th Annual Burgee Reunion, noon until evening." "Let's get together and keep that family spirit alive." "We plan to have a Pot Luck Lunch around 1:00, and bring a dish to share." "Remember those goodies we always have . . . . keep them coming." "We will provide paper products, iced tea and coffee, strawberries and ice cream, and a new treat . . . snow cones." "We have lots of fun activities planned for the afternoon, and please don't forget the HAYRIDE!" "It would be fun if everybody brought old photographs or old stories of times past." "Let's have a big crowd this year. See you soon." Yes, fun was had by all.

It has been about thirty years since Hurricane Agnes roared out of the Gulf of Mexico, hitting all of the states from Florida to New York. I recall that the storm caused 19 inches of rain to fall, and 122 persons were reported killed, 21 killed in Maryland. The reason I remember these details is due to the fact that my family picked that exact time to vacation in Orlando, Florida. The Robertson family joined us on this June trip from Westminster, MD, to Orlando, FL, and we filled two station wagons. Our exposure to Disney World, Sea World, Universal Studios, and other attractions needs no detailed comments, but let me say that Agnes did not dampen our enjoyment. In fact, I did not sense the scope of the storm's damage until our return home, arriving at the foot of our driveway late at night.

Our station wagon reached Westminster about 11:00 at night, and the Agnes storm of 1972 had passed through just days earlier. We were tired from the long Florida trip, and every family member desired to fall into bed. The sight before us was hard to believe. Our long driveway had a barricade across it, and the car's lights revealed the extent of the storm damage. We would be forced to carry belongings up the driveway in order to reach our house. Had the barricade not been there, our car would have fallen into a ditch which was 6 feet wide and 5 feet deep, extending across the entire road. My wife's father, Dr. Jennette, had anticipated the danger we faced, and he had the barricade erected. It took a week for us to close the gaping hole at the bottom of our driveway, and the dirt road leading up to our house had to be paved. Our family members did not add to the death toll of Agnes, but we will remember our difficult late night walk up a country lane in June of 1972, a walk up a lane that had been washed away by a storm named Agnes.

EVENTS PRIOR TO THE FOREIGN CAR INVASION:

A Rotarian friend's Pontiac Tempest

It was perhaps in 1974 that a Rotarian friend of mine passed away, and his family wanted me to have printed material related to Rotary International. One item was a printed Code of Ethics, protected in a large picture frame. The code is highly prized by Rotarians, seen as a guide to proper business behavior. The McLaughlin family also asked if I was interested in owning the Pontiac Tempest that was parked in their garage. A mechanic friend verified that the car was in excellent condition, so we purchased the car at a very reasonable price, making it one of our two family cars. At that time, we were adjusting to life in our first Westminster home, and Carol generally drove the large Pontiac station wagon, a driver training car that we purchased from another member of my Rotary club. In 1974, I had access to a college owned car for my college admissions travel duties, which mainly covered a five-state area, visiting high schools during the months of September, October, and November.

Driving the light blue Tempest was a real joy for me, and I liked the size of the car and I liked its good mileage. The Tempest was attractive, but I do recall that the car possessed what might be described as a tiny flaw. On occasion, the rear trunk lid would pop open, revealing my supply of college admission's pamphlets and Western Maryland College catalogues. The latch would sometimes not catch firmly, and a few times the lid swung open while I was driving down a highway. The contents of the trunk would fly out on to the road if I did not stop rapidly. My use

51

of the car was mainly limited to Maryland destinations, and Carol's larger car was used for longer family trips, especially those vacation trips to Ocean City, Maryland.

An April Fool's Day happening

In 1975, on April Fool's Day, the Office of the Western Maryland College President called me, suggesting that I move my car. The car was apparently obstructing traffic. I had no idea what this was all about, but I left the Admissions Office to check on the Tempest. Imagine my surprise when I found it parked on the sidewalk, making it difficult for students to enter the front door of the College Library. At this point, it became clear that some member of my admissions staff had played an April fool's joke on me, and somehow the College President had agreed to go along with the plan. How my staff member got access to my car keys remains a mystery, and most of my office staff, until now, never heard "the rest of the story."

When President Ralph John agreed to take part in the April Fool's Day joke of 1975, he also knew that he and I had recently had our one and only difficult encounter. The point of friction resulted because Maryland State legislators asked me to testify on certain proposed scholarship legislation, and Maryland's Governor Mandel had asked President John to block my testimony in Annapolis on those bills. As an officer in the local admissions and financial aid organizations, I was expected to appear and testify, but I told President John I would stay away from Annapolis if that was what he wanted me to do. He gave me no such order, so I went to testify, agreeing to make it clear that my testimony was not in any way an expression of the views of Western Maryland College, my employer. This I did, but Governor Mandel immediately notified Dr. John of his displeasure, and President John then passed the criticism on to me, saying that I had gone against his instructions. At this very moment, in April of 1975, I was weighing a job offer to head the Maryland State Scholarship Board, so I backed away from any further argument with President

Ralph John over the Annapolis testimony affair. Now with this disclosure, you and my former admissions staff know "the rest of the story."

A new job provided a new car in 1975

Bobby Taubman has been a very dear friend for many years, and in 1975, he urged me to leave my admissions post at Western Maryland College to run the Maryland State Scholarship Program. Bobby was Chairman of the Scholarship Board at that time, and numerous changes were needed if the students of Maryland were to be better served by the State funded scholarship programs. Leaving the College that I loved was a most difficult decision, but I accepted the challenge of the new State position, and I held that post for the next decade, the years 1975-1985.

During my decade in the State Scholarship office, there were many worthy accomplishments, but I'll list only a few. The office was computerized for the first time, all prior work having been done by hand. By extending the time period for awarding grants to students, those budgeted funds that had previously been reverted back to the State as unused funds were now being fully used by students to pay college bills. I helped to write and implement the first Distinguished Scholar Program of Maryland, honoring the brightest high school graduates and giving them grants if they attended a college in Maryland. In 1980, the Maryland public television station accepted my suggestion to initiate a program which would address the ways college students could obtain aid to pay the costs of higher education. I worked with the station staff to produce *You Can Afford College*, and I'm proud to say that that program started in January of 1981 is still running in year 2012. Also, in my decade at the Maryland Scholarship Board, training programs were conducted in the Annapolis State House for Maryland legislators and staff members to learn how State awards fit into the total college financial aid picture. The first federally-funded SSIG money coming to Maryland was started in this same decade, and in 1985, I was honored to be National President of all state scholarship programs in the United States.

A car was assigned to me early in the decade of my service to the State, and it did make it easier for me to attend legislative sessions held in Annapolis. My frequent use of the car to visit high school and college campuses was also a time-saving benefit, thus no longer requiring me to request a transportation vehicle from some State car pool in the Baltimore area. It was a saving of time and effort for me to travel directly from my home to the desired destination rather than starting and stopping each journey at a car pool location. The State car was never intended to be used as a "Family vehicle," but it nonetheless did reduce my need to use our other family owned cars.

Autos in the later years (since 1990)

A return to classroom teaching and a city home

When I concluded my decade as Executive Director of the Maryland State Scholarship Board in 1985, hasty calculations revealed that I had about ten more years of employment before retirement. There were numerous new areas of interest that I wanted to investigate, but all sensible advice coming my way seemed to be directing me back into positions in which I had many years of experience. My decision was made to return to high school teaching in 1986, and this classroom duty would correspond to my first employment position held in Madison High School some 32 years earlier. My return to teaching mathematics and coaching the girls' tennis team at Westminster High would bring me great pleasure, if not a large salary. I refer you back to page 28 which shows my first teaching contract in 1954, and the starting salary at that time may surprise you.

A foreign car invasion thanks to "Ick":

A Mercedes Benz for Carol

In the 1990s, my wife received a phone call from Ick, the mechanic who had serviced our family cars for many years. The call was about a car she might be interested in buying. A few years earlier, Ick had talked me into buying a slightly used BMW, and I urged her to accept his advice. Although Carol dearly loved the Volvo that she had driven for many years, the Mercedes was a deal we could not resist. At first, Carol said: "If I drive around town in a

Mercedes, people will think I'm showing off." After her quick adjustment to the beautiful new car, I joked with her, asking: "Why are you extending your left hand out of the car's window like the Queen of England if you do not want to attract attention?" The Mercedes did look brand

new, but, in reality, it was about three to four years old, and it had Ick's full recommendation. In the photo (shown above), Ick and Carol are standing by the Mercedes, and the auto shop behind them is the International Foreign Car Service Center. Ick is the proud owner of this highly successful business, and his advice about which cars to buy has been our guide for over 25 years. He is a true friend and he has our complete trust. Ick came to our country in 1974 from Uganda, and his full name is Iqubal Moledina.

Shadow dog's trip to Wake Forest University

Now that Carol's Mercedes and my BMW were our two family vehicles, it was decided that we would take the Mercedes on any long trip and my slightly older BMW would remain at home in the garage. Actually, both cars were always garage protected from the time we acquired them. Seldom did they ever have to sit outside to face the heat of the sun or to encounter the bitter winter weather. When we journeyed to Williamsburg, VA, for our annual Christmas visit, our dog, Shadow, could not join us in the Mercedes because our time-share locations did not allow pets. He could join us on other occasions, and one such trip was our visit to Wake Forest University for Carol's class reunion.

After meeting Shadow for the first time in the year 2007, I wrote the following: Shadow was the most perfect physical specimen of a dog that I had ever seen. Our past Labs had been mostly blondes, and never had they weighed more than 40-50 pounds. Shadow had the size of a small thoroughbred horse, carrying well over 100 pounds on his strong legs. He had a black shinny coat and beautiful white markings on his chest and on all four paws. A colorful kerchief was attached to his powerful neck, making him look like a Christmas package. My dog leach, which was for a dog in the 60-80 pound range, would not do the job. When he jumped up to lick my face, I fell back several feet, reminding me of my high school football days. Had veterinarian Dr. Herrick been present, I may have reconsidered taking Shadow home with me that day. Shadow came with his own crate, one that he seemed to have outgrown, and I questioned if the need was for a stable rather than a crate.

The six or seven hour trip to North Carolina was quite comfortable in the Mercedes, and Shadow filled the back seat as he slept. When not sleeping or reaching through the seats to kiss our cheeks, he moved from window to window. In case I had not yet mentioned it, Shadow (shown below using a baby crib to improve his view of the outside world) is 115 pounds of Lab and Great Dane mixed, resembling a small horse. If Carol was driving, she would often say that she

wished he would sit down so that he would not block her view in the rear-view mirror. My answer to Carol's wish was generally the same: "Carol, he is sitting down." We checked Into an Inn near the Wake Forest campus and our third floor room required that shadow enter and exit by the main lobby, a bit of a surprise to other guests registering for rooms. Shadow liked the use of the elevators, but he sometimes hit the wrong elevator buttons. When the room was to be serviced by the maid, we left Shadow in his crate, knowing that he would be too friendly to room visitors. All went well, and many Inn employees will never forget Shadow's brief stay.

A 1988 BMW caught Ken's eye

The year must have been 1990 when I received an important phone call from Ick of the International Foreign Car Service in Westminster. He wanted me to know that he was servicing a 1988 BMW for a medical doctor, and, if I was interested, the doctor might be willing to sell it to me. Ick knew that I preferred to buy cars that were two to three years old rather than purchase brand new cars, and he also knew that my current automobile was about ready for replacement. When Ick recommended a car, he knew that I trusted his judgment, and he did all of the work on our family cars.

When I stopped at the Green Street garage to see the BMW, you could say that it was love at first sight for me. It was everything I could want in a car. It looked brand new, because it had been driven only 9000 miles. My photo with the car is shown below. More than four years still remained on the doctor's seven-year warranty when I bought the car. I loved the silver-gold color, and the car was the perfect size, not too large and not too small. It had a very short turning radius, and the standard shift provided excellent gas mileage. I would be able to buy the BMW for about half of its original selling price, and Ick had been the person who serviced the car regularly for the car's first owner. Little did I know that I would still be driving that same car twenty-two years later as my primary vehicle, and that many people would still be complimenting me on the nice looking car that I was driving in the year 2011.

A "gift-car" led to a difficult BMW decision

For many years, Carol and I have been close friends of the Frank Libman family, and in their later years, Frank and his wife, Sophie, needed Carol to join them on some of their travels, some trips inside the United States and others outside of the country. Sophie was losing her eye sight, and Carol was considered the perfect companion for her. After Sophie passed away, especially when Frank's age was nearing ninety, Carol's services continued to be needed, and her dedication to Frank was like that of a devoted daughter. She drove Frank's car whenever he called on her help, driving him to local and distant points. Frank decided that his Ford car should be placed in Carol's name, so his unexpected gift to Carol provided us with a third car. Unfortunately, our Westminster home's garage that was built to hold two cars, and the additional Ford

would force us to keep one family car outside at all times. The BMW deserved no such fate, so I decided that my beloved car should be sold. I had been driving the 1988 BMW for more than two decades, and it was very hard for me to part with the vehicle that had become such a loyal and dependable member of the Shook household.

Our Shook home (pictured above) is currently located on the corner of Washington Road and Stoner Avenue, and in the year 2011, my 1988 BMW was often parked on the Stoner Avenue side of the house. A few "For Sale" signs were attached, and the immediate interest in the BMW came as no surprise to me. The heavy traffic flow gave the car a lot of exposure, and the car looked almost like new. While in my possession, it was always kept in a garage and out of the weather, and its 235,000 miles was as indication that it still had a long life ahead of it.

Since a Maryland inspection would be required before any new owner could drive the BMW, I decided to pay for such an inspection myself. To my surprise, the inspection said that the BMW needed to have repair work directed at numerous rust spots on the underside of the car. The car ran beautifully, but rust had resulted from snow and salt lodged under the car during the cold winter months. When the one person showing the greatest interest in the BMW could not locate a repair shop that would do the work at a reasonable price, I decided to retain the car for six to nine months, and then I would donate it to some worthy charity. I would drive the BMW on a daily basis, and Carol would divide her driving time between the Ford and the Mercedes. I apologized to the BMW that it would need to be parked outside for the next nine months.

My BMW gift to breast cancer research

What could be called a medical emergency forced me to change my plans for use of the BMW. On Thursday, July 28, 2011, I drove my BMW to York, PA, for a medical session, and I had trouble walking the short distance from the car to the medical office. The right leg would not function properly, and this had never occurred before. The medical staff checked me over and the findings shocked me. It seems that my four known aneurisms on the aorta were not the problem, but it was discovered that my right artery was not delivering blood to my right leg. Since the main doctor at the York facility could not be scheduled to see me until the following Monday, I returned to my home in Westminster and arranged a Friday appointment with my family doctor, Dr. Galvin. On my drive home from York, PA, in the BMW, I had to lift my right leg to place it on the brake pedal or to place it on the gas pedal. I concluded that my right leg difficulty would no longer allow me to drive a standard shift car, and the BMW was standard shift.

At my Friday appointment, Dr. Galvin felt that my right leg was cold and he immediately sent me to the Carroll County Hospital. Shortly thereafter, an operation took place to connect my left artery to the right leg, thus providing the blood the right leg needed. Any longer delay in the blood flow could have cost me a foot or a portion of the leg. The portion of the artery with the blood clot was by-passed, and no effort was therefore needed to clean out the blockage.

On Tuesday, November 8, 2011, a large tow truck arrived at my home to take away my BMW. A breast cancer research group was happy to receive my car donation. Our Ford station wagon just happened to be parked across from my garage when the tow truck driver tried to attach the BMW to her truck. As strange as it sounds, the BMW broke loose from the tow truck and it backed down the street. Although it drifted slowly, it bumped into the side of our Ford, putting a slight dent into the right rear door. I tell people that the BMW was getting even with the Ford for pushing it out of the Shook family. The charity group reported that the BMW was quickly sold, and I hope it found a nice new home.

PART II

DISTANT TRAVELS TRIGGER MEMOIRS

PART II – DISTANT TRAVELS TRIGGER MEMOIRS

A FAMILY MEMBER WAS A TRAVEL AGENT:

My daughter, Jennette, became a travel agent after her graduation from Gettysburg College, and she has been able to share some of her low-cost travel opportunities with her parents. In the first photo that follows, Jennette and I are enjoying the company of President Thomas Jefferson in Williamsburg, VA, and in the second photograph, Jennette is standing with a Turkish friend in front of a Turkish mosque in Istanbul. This second photo was taken during her 1982-83 school year in which she continued her studies in Istanbul, Turkey.

After her high school graduation in Westminster, MD, Jennette applied to study overseas on a student exchange program, and she was shocked to be assigned to a country whose language was unknown to her. Told not to take her best clothing, because she might live with a poor family, she later wrote for her better clothing. She would live with the Yesil family of Tarabya, a community just north of Istanbul. Her new parents were owners of factories and the presence of a family yacht seemed to indicate a well-to-do family. Only the young Yesil daughter, Emel, spoke English, and Jennette and Emel would become life-long friends.

My fond trip to Turkey in 1996

My trip to Turkey with Jennette in 1996 was an unforgettable event, and equally impressive was our trip, taken in 1998, to see the many wonders of Egypt. In a letter dated May 17, 1996, I sent the following remarks to a few relatives and close friends:

I have been back in Westminster, Maryland, for almost two months since my trip to Turkey, and letters to special people about this remarkable experience are long overdue. Jennette, who shared this trip with me, calls often from her home in Quakertown, Pennsylvania, and she is still talking about her memorable return trip to Turkey. She was an exchange student in Istanbul some thirteen years ago, and many of her former friends went far out of their way to welcome us. I agree that Turkey has wondrous sights that everyone should see, but I have to say that Jennette's friends were equally impressive. These young people were very friendly and quite generous with their time and money. When I attempted to pay for their tea or boat rides, they said with a laugh that my money was no good. I was their guest, and I would have the opportunity to pay when they visited us in the United States.

I can say that I enjoyed all 17 days of the trip, and I had eight hours of film to prove it. After a full week in Istanbul, we joined our scheduled tour and visited Ankara, the capital of Turkey. The tour then continued south to the Cappadocia Region, followed by Antalya and world-famous Ephesus. Jennette and I were given nice gifts by her friends, but we also purchased such items as tiles, rugs, tee shirts, silver jewelry, evil-eye key rings (to protect us), and a musical instrument called a soz. Take my word for it, carrying the soz home on the plane is not an experience that I will soon want to repeat.

Back in the United States, I have had a number of opportunities to speak to local Rotary clubs about the Turkey trip, and club members are interested in hearing about a country that few have visited. I acquainted them with the friendly people, the history, and the remarkable ancient ruins found in Turkey. I mentioned that I walked on the streets of Istanbul late at night, and I felt safer than I would have felt walking the streets of Baltimore City or Washington, DC. Within the 30 minute time frame for a talk, I did mention that Turkey had problems with neighboring countries. Greece, Iraq, and Armenia are examples of problem neighbors. Greece tried to restrict Turkey's access to waterways that had always been available, and Iraq allowed terrorists to hide on its side of the border, directing sneak attacks against communities on the Turkish side. Turkey still remains a democracy as it faces such hostilities.

In closing, I point out certain locations that visitors to Turkey must visit. Istanbul has historic mosques and palaces that must be seen, and I especially liked the Blue Mosque. The Grand Bazaar with its 3000 shops must be part of any tour, and a boat ride up the Bosporus Strait to the Black Sea is enjoyable, viewing Europe on the left side (west) and Asia on the right (east). In Ankara, the two main attractions are the Museum and Ataturk's Mausoleum. Ataturk made Turkey a democracy in 1923 and became the country's first president. His picture is on most printed money, and his photo is on many street corners and in most school rooms. The Cappadocia Region is where it is said that 150,000 Christians and others seeking safety lived in underground cities or lived far above the ground in shelters dug into the face of volcanic rock formations, some called "Fairy Chimneys."

On the southern edge of Turkey, you arrive at a popular tourist spot for many Europeans. This spot on the Mediterranean is called Antalya with lovely beaches and even snow-capped mountains. Moving west, we reach the remarkable ancient city of Ephesus, a Roman city which dates back more than 2000 years. Seeing statues and relics in museums can never match the experience of actually walking the same streets that inhabitants walked 2000 years earlier.

A trip that travel agents cannot duplicate

As I mentioned above, Jennette and I also enjoyed a trip to Egypt, thanks to her role as a travel agent. That trip appears as a memoir in my first memoir book, *Getting Hooked on Memoirs*. The trip to Egypt was 2-3 weeks in length, and the price was reasonable, especially since travel agent discounts were available to us. Also appearing in my book, *Getting Hooked on Memoirs*, a book that was published in July of 2011, is my memoir account of a trip that I enjoyed in 1992, a Rotary sponsored trip to New Zealand. That trip allowed me and five other non-Rotarians to spend five weeks in the Wellington area of New Zealand. While staying on the north island of New Zealand, we acted as US ambassadors, learning their culture and sharing with them our own life experiences. We lived in the homes of Rotarians, and our activities ranged from visits to sessions of Parliament to the shearing of sheep and dancing and grunting with the historic Maori groups. As for their humor, an old gentleman said, "Every retired man needs a car, a TV, and a wife, and they should all be working." When I shared this with my wife back in the US, she immediately quit her job. My daughter looked over our full New Zealand agenda, and she concluded that her travel agency could not duplicate the Group Study Exchange trip of Rotary for any amount of money. It was truly a once-in-a-lifetime type of experience.

NATIONAL ASSOCIATIONS COVERED THE USA

My many years of employment in the fields of college admissions and college student financial aid caused me to hold membership in these four national associations: the College Entrance Examination Board (CEEB), the National Association of College Admissions Counselors (NACAC), the National Association of State Scholarship and Grant Programs (NASSGP), and the National Association of Student Financial Aid Administrators (NASFAA).

Dr. H. Kenneth Shook

NASSGP

National Association of State Scholarship and Grant Programs

July 7, 1985

President
H. Kenneth Shook
Maryland State Scholarship Board
2100 Guilford Avenue
Baltimore, Maryland 21218
(301) 659-6420

President-Elect
John E. Madigan
Rhode Island Higher Education Assistance Authority
274 Weybosset Street
Providence, Rhode Island 02903
(401) 277-2050

Secretary
R. Ross Erbschloe
Arizona Commission for Postsecondary Education
1645 W. Jefferson
Phoenix, Arizona 85009
(602) 255-3109

Treasurer
Debra Wiley
Colorado Commission on Higher Education
Colorado Heritage Center
1300 Broadway, 2nd Floor
Denver, Colorado 80203
(303) 866-2748

Past President
Gary K. Weeks
Legislative Fiscal Office
H178 State Capitol
Salem, Oregon
(503) 378-5152

Council Member
Gary W. Nichols
Iowa College Aid Commission
201 Jewett Building
Ninth and Grand Avenues
Des Moines, Iowa 50309
(515) 281-3501

Council Member

The Honorable William Ford
Chairman
Subcommittee on Postsecondary Education
Committee on Education and Labor
United States House of Representatives
Washington, D.C. 20515

Dear Mr. Chairman:

Attached are the position papers of the National Association of State Scholarship and Grant Programs. The Reauthorization Proposal for State Student Incentive Grant Program was officially accepted by the Association at our business meeting on June 6, 1985.

As President of NASSGP, I am pleased to testify in behalf of the continuation of SSIG. This student aid program truly symbolizes the best aspects of a desired federal-state partnership in helping financially needy students. The SSIG program has proven its worth, and future expansion of funding levels can certainly be justified.

Sincerely,

H. Kenneth Shook
NASSGP President

A sample NASSGP letter which appears above shows my contact with the Chairman of the Subcommittee on Postsecondary Education in 1985. Washington visits were a necessity at that time as I met with legislative committees in my capacity as President of NASSGP. My membership in national groups covered the years 1958-1985, and the annual meetings took us to most of the major cities in the United States, from Seattle and San Diego in the west to cities such as New York and Washington, DC, in the east.

The cities were memorable, but one's active participation in the groups is what triggered the fondest memories. My numerous research papers were printed in the journals of CEEB and NACAC, and I was honored to serve as National President of NASSGP in 1985.

INTERNATIONAL ASSOCIATIONS COVER THE WORLD:

While national association trips took me to many desirable locations in the United States, my membership in Rotary took me to spots in many parts of the world. Without Rotary, I doubt that I would have visited such places as Singapore, Brisbane, Quito, and Wellington. The visit to Wellington, New Zealand, was part of Rotary's Group Study Exchange Program, and my travel agent daughter said that her agency could not have duplicated that five-week trip at any price. Another trip she said she could not duplicate was my trip to Copenhagen, Denmark, that included a side trip to Norway and its impressive fiords. That trip was arranged under a Rotary program called a Family Friendship Exchange.

Group Study Exchange became a program of the Rotary Foundation in 1965, and nearly 500 teams travel annually to other parts of the world, visiting a Rotary District for about five weeks. Since Rotary International is composed of over 500 districts, the Foundation pairs up districts each year for the exchange. Our Maryland district, for example, might send a team this year to a district in India, and the following year we might exchange teams with a district in Norway. I was selected from a group of fifteen Rotarian applicants to be the GSE Team Leader in 1992 for our Rotary District, District 7620. Our GSE team would visit New Zealand. Another Rotary program allows Rotary families to exchange visits with Rotary families in other parts of the world. This program has existed since the 1980s, and it is understood that participants should reciprocate, allowing visits to flow between districts, not just in one direction.

In the first photograph, Carol and I are seen with host families as we tour Copenhagen, and in the second picture, Carol and I are standing in front of the Hans Christian Andersen home. All individuals, both young and old, must surely remember those Andersen tales which include: *The Ugly Duckling*, *Thumbelina*, and the all-time favorite story of *The Little Mermaid*.

My wife could not join me on the New Zealand trip, but she did share the Denmark trip. She has also joined me at numerous conventions of Rotary International. Rotary's Family Friendship Exchange allows Rotary families to visit with families in another part of the world, and afterwards, it is understood that families from that Rotary district will come to the sending district to reciprocate the earlier visits. The plan is to stay in the homes of Rotarians, and the host families will conduct local tours

After a busy day touring Copenhagen, the local Rotarians treated us to a night at the Royal Ballet. Tickets were sold out, but kind Rotarians donated their tickets to us. My seat was in the first row of the balcony, right next to the Royal box. To my regret, the Queen did not attend that night's performance. Had she attended, I was prepared to tell her that I had met her father, King Frederick, when I visited Denmark many years earlier, in 1957. King Frederick had passed me while I stood in front of his Summer Palace, and he said, "Good morning" to me in perfect English. A Dane, who happened to be standing nearby, informed me that my greeter was none other than the King of Denmark. King Frederick was walking to his car, and I was told he often drove alone during his travels around his country. If I had met King Frederick's daughter at the ballet, that would have added nicely to the Denmark memoir.

Dr. H. Kenneth Shook

The 1997 photo shown above pictures eight male Rotarians who had served as Governors of District 7620, a District area covering that portion of Maryland which lies west of the Chesapeake Bay and also including Washington, DC. I quickly add that in the years that followed 1997, some female Rotarians have served as Governors of this District. I also add that it has been my experience that Rotarians serving as District Governors (DGs) are the Rotarians that benefit the most from the programs of this international organization. Presidents of local clubs surely benefit from their time in office, but far too often these local officers miss the joy of activity on the international stage. I now share with you three of my international experiences in Rotary.

A Yachting Fellowship experience

The first memorable experience I'd like to share took place on my trip to the annual conference of Rotary International held in Brisbane, Australia, in June of 2003. While at the conference, members of the Rotary Yachting Fellowship added Carol and Ken Shook to their roster, and I believe that $10 was our only charge. To sweeten the bargain, we were offered a ride on a yacht when we passed through the Hawaiian Islands on our way home the very next week. Before the flight to Oahu, Carol and I enjoyed the spectacular harbor of Sydney, Australia. I tried to convince Carol to walk across the top of the Sydney Bridge, but she refused.

Some three days later, we arrived in Oahu and did a quick tour of Pearl Harbor. Visits were made to the USS Arizona Memorial and the USS Missouri. The photograph above shows Carol and I standing on the very spot where the Japanese surrendered, bringing World War II to a close. A plaque now appears at that spot on the wooden deck of the USS Missouri. Our Rotary friends were happy to receive our phone call, and a ride on their yacht was arranged for the next day. The ride took about three hours, and cheese and wine were served to all on board. Two other guests were in the small group, and we were surprised to learn their backgrounds. The one Rotarian was local, and he had repaired the clock damaged by Japanese aircraft when they attacked Pearl Harbor in December of 1941. That clock's tower is located near the entry to the Harbor. The other Rotarian guest on the yacht said he had been a German submarine captain in World War II, and he shared his experiences, none of which took place in the Pacific Ocean. We sailed to the entrance of Pearl Harbor, but the yacht was not allowed to enter the restricted area. This yachting experience was another great Rotary event in my life.

The Rotary Convention in San Antonia

I missed the RI Convention of 2000 because both knees were being replaced on the same June morning in Westminster, Maryland. Dr. Blue did a perfect job on the knees, but while attending rehab on the knees in York, PA, I was hit with a different medical emergency. Four aneurisms on my aorta caused me to have a second operation, and that led to my white light experience. The account of that near-death happening is a memoir reported in my previous book, *Getting Hooked on Memoirs*. By June of 2001, I was eager to travel to San Antonio for the 2001 RI Convention. The Convention Center and the River Walk were the perfect setting for such a meeting, and about 25,000 people attended the event. Frank Devlyn of Mexico City was the RI President that year, and the flags of all countries having Rotary clubs were delivered to the Convention by riders on horseback. It was a great way to open the festivities.

On my flight to the Convention, I had a stop in Atlanta, GA, and my recovering knees earned me the right to have access to a restricted waiting area. I seemed to be alone when I sat on two rows of benches placed back to back. I may have been partly asleep when the head of the person seated behind me rocked and collided with my head. I walked to the other side of the benches to see if the other person was injured, and I was shocked to see Ray Charles seated there, listening to taped music. Since he had no sight, I tapped him on the knee and asked if his head was okay. He apologized for rocking his head far enough back to hit me, and said he had a habit of such head motions even during concerts. Later as I entered the plane for San Antonio, I walked past him in the first class section of the plane, and now his male companion was at his side. Imagine bumping heads with Ray Charles?

Before leaving my home town in Maryland for the flight to San Antonio, I should have obtained the phone number and address of Susan Smith. Susie was a former choir director of the Methodist Church in Westminster, and she was the only person I knew who lived in the San Antonio area. She was no longer married, so Smith was no longer her last name. As you might have expected, I arrived at the RI Convention location with absolutely no way to find Susie among the thousands of residents of San Antonio, and, not being a Rotarian, she would not be at the Convention. Believe it or not, I spoke to her within five minutes of arriving at the Convention. Entering the building, a Rotarian from my home District passed me and said a woman who knows me is selling ties in the first booth of our display hall. Sure enough, there in the first booth of several hundred booths was Susie Smith. She was helping a friend on just that first day to sell ties to Rotarians. After the Convention ended, Susie and I had time for a lunch together before my flight left for home. Thus, I had two amazing encounters on this one trip to the 2001 RI Convention.

"Songs for Rotarians" is #1 on Google lists

When I was preparing to become District Governor of District 7620 of Rotary International, I journeyed to California to be trained with hundreds of other Rotarians from all parts of the world. Even the spouses were invited to receive their own special training sessions. Over the years, I joke that my wife did not heed the training advice, because she never threw flower petals to mark my pathway. It was a custom for incoming governors to give small gifts to the others in that same training class, so I gave an original laminated song as my gift. I'm told that my gift had never been duplicated by any previous incoming governor. From that beginning, I eventually produced enough songs to form a song book called, "Songs for Rotarians." One version of the book, a revision of December 2004, still appears at the top of page one for two Google listings, "Rotary songs" and "Rotary singing." I am often asked how and why my book has held such a lofty position on Google for nearly a decade, and I can only guess at the answer. The book is unique in that music and lyrics can be down-loaded, and each song provides a history behind it. Also, most living Past-Presidents of Rotary International have written me about the book, and their quotations appear in the book. The one song that generated the greatest response was titled *What All Rotarians Know*, and the history of that song that is in the song book is as follows:

WHAT ALL ROTARIANS KNOW (Twenty Rotary International themes) was first written in 2002, and it has been modified several times since. Rotary International themes have always impressed me, and I enjoyed using some of the themes during my District Governor year, such as "Put life into Rotary, your life." Since shorter themes could be more easily arranged with the tune I developed, I had to reject lengthy themes, and I focused on themes of recent years. Two verses seemed like a logical stopping point, until some Rotarian said that the 2002-2003 theme, "Sow the seeds of love," should also be included. That led to the writing of verse three and the need for another four themes. The theme of Luis Giay, "Build the future with action and vision," concluded verse three, increasing the number of song themes to fifteen. Raja Saboo sent a nice note saying, "You seem to be immortalizing the Past-Presidents, at least their themes," and Richard King's office praised the effort. Luis Giay wrote that he liked the song, and he said "We are looking forward to sharing this work with our Rotary club." Jim Lacy wrote, "Ken, your song is good, but where is *Follow your Rotary dream?* Needless to say, I took Jim's advice and added a fourth verse to the song to include his theme. After this action, the revised song contained a total of twenty RI themes. I am pleased that the themes of Jim Lacy, Frank Devlyn, and Charlie Keller could be included in the final verse. I dedicate this song to two Past-Presidents, Richard King and Cliff Dochterman, whose fine themes have honored positions in the first verse of *WHAT ALL ROTARIANS KNOW*.

The demanding District Governor role

When I stated earlier that the District Governor role opens the door for a greater enjoyment of Rotary and a greater involvement in its many programs, I had no doubt that the observation was a correct one, but there are some exceptions to this conclusion. I know that in some instances the demands of holding such a Rotary position can cause personal difficulties. Persons not yet retired can find that their non-Rotary obligations suffer, and, in some cases, serious health conditions emerge. In my District 7620, a Governor must plan to visit all clubs (about 65 in number) within a five-month span, and the area covered includes all of central Maryland and Washington, DC. Some clubs hold morning meetings, and these can make travel difficult for a Governor who faces the increased traffic of commuters heading to work. The District Governor in Alaska has been known to visit clubs in many time zones, and in some areas of the world, Governors have to fly to clubs they cannot reach by automobile. Also, some Governors finance much of their Rotary expenses, while in other districts, budgets are quite adequate. Since I was retired prior to my DG year in 1997-1998 and my budget was adequate, I found my Rotary experiences to be filled with joy, and to this day, Rotary remains a big part of my life.

PART III

MEMOIRS TRIGGER OTHER MEMOIRS

Part III – Memoirs Trigger Other Memoirs

Exchanging memoirs over morning coffee:

A perfect start to the new day must include a tasty breakfast, in my opinion, and on most mornings, I eat my breakfast at one of the local restaurants. After retiring from my work schedule in 1995, it seemed natural for me to look for a morning coffee group to join. Becoming a member of such a group did require a certain obligation, but 100% attendance was never a requirement for membership. The first group to gain my attention was a Baugher's Restaurant gathering of friends of Charlie Havens. Charlie was a former coach at Western Maryland College, and most coffee group members had also been employees of that College. Charlie and I had also been members of the Westminster Rotary Club, and I decided to join his morning group. Jack Molesworth, Victor Makovich, Brom Watkins, and others attended the daily meetings to eat and to share fond memories of past years. The first of the two attached photos shows an aging Charlie Havens at one of his last coffee group appearances, and after his death, the Baugher's Restaurant group slowly dissolved.

Two coffee groups met at the local Roy Rogers Restaurant, and one tended to be a golf group while the other was composed mainly of retired farmers. I sampled both groups, and I suggested that each group display the morning topics for discussion on a bulletin board. My suggestion was not followed, but I did divide my time between the two groups.

Dr. H. Kenneth Shook

One morning at Roy Rogers, an oriental fellow was ahead of me in line when he was asked if he wanted his saddle bags packed for the trail. The young fellow behind the counter taking the order was dressed in western garb, and I could tell that the customer in front of me did not understand the question being asked. I stepped to his aid and said he needed to respond if the order was to be taken out or to be eaten in the restaurant. Later, the episode triggered great laughter in my coffee group.

In the year 2002, I discovered two coffee groups at the local McDonald's Restaurant. One group was discussing a topic of interest to me, the decision made by the Western Maryland College Board of Trustees to change the College's name. Since I knew all of the details of the controversial decision, I was pulled into that coffee group, and ten years later, I still remained a loyal member. During the decade, some members died and one member, Helen Franklin, entered the Copper Ridge Retirement Home. Ed and Tina Gribbens are new to the group, and members that carry over from the earlier group include: Nancy and Bob Reppe, Ken and Mary Lou Martin, Howell and Hilda Schnauble, Mrs. Karl Zepp, Charles Sluder, and Harry Brown. Many are pictured in the attached photo of the group visiting Helen Franklin in her retirement home. Helen is third from the right, and her daughter is to her right side.

The age range for the members of our McDonald's coffee group perhaps extends from those in their sixties to those willing to admit to being in their nineties. I suppose that Hal Schnauble is the oldest at age 93, but he doesn't look a day over 92 ½. He looks young enough to work, but when asked to join in some reasonable yard work, he always replies: Don't hold your breath! Men constitute about 90% of the regular members, and Wednesdays have been recognized as mornings to welcome our spouses for coffee and possibly cake. New members are welcome, and the application for membership does not require an attached photograph.

The McDonald's coffee group continues to be active in year 2012, but the group becomes quite small when three couples spend the winter months in Florida. The daily discussion topics seldom change. Sports and weather are of interest, and politics and taxation levels are ever present. A few stock market items are checked on a daily basis, and I remind Howell of his bad advice on several stocks. Harry shares old photos from his file collection, and we all conclude that he was quite a lady's man in his younger years. Charlie shares his medical knowledge, and I offer information on higher education issues. Humor is also a daily menu item and we never let Ken Martin forget the day at McDonald's when he ordered and received a cinnamon bun made of plastic. Ken pointed to the item that looked good in the glass case, but he and the server did not realize the error until Ken broke his knife trying to cut it. Howell gets a laugh when he wears a shirt with a photo on it, picturing the members of the original coffee group, and everyone has fun watching Howell try to break the coffee plastic stirrer in the middle. His daily efforts fail by as much as a half inch, and the "boo-birds" can be heard.

Of the many jokes shared in the group, I'd say that the "little red fire truck" joke is the most popular. As the story goes, a farmer concluded that his barn was a total loss when the big fire companies backed their trucks away and attached yellow lines between the trees to keep people a safe distance from the blaze. At that point, a small rural station fire truck arrived on the scene and crashed through the yellow lines. When it stopped near the barn, men jumped off the truck and began fighting the fire. Others became inspired, and they too joined in the effort to save the barn. The barn was saved, and the farmer showed his gratitude by giving a $1,000 check to the driver of the rural fire house truck. When asked how the money would be spent, he responded: "To fix the damm breaks on that truck!"

The reactions of the individuals in my coffee group to my membership in Rotary with its ethical code of good conduct were what one would expect, and I often needed to remind them that memoirs must be reported exactly as they occur, and that the personal accounts must be truthful. A visitor from the other McDonald's coffee group played on this theme when he heard me say that my grandmother did a lot of sewing and that she always broke the tread with her teeth. She used thimbles but never scissors. This fellow, a Mr. Green, said he once visited a farm, and a button flew off of his pants. A repair was needed, since he was not wearing a belt at the time. He asked the farmer's wife for a safety pin to hold up his pants. She insisted on sewing the button on his pants, and he did not need to disrobe. Mr. Green appreciated the fact that she did the repair while her husband was out of the kitchen, but just as she bent down to break the thread with her teeth, he returned through the kitchen door. Mr. Green claimed he had never been more embarrassed in his life.

Photographs of a man and his dog

There are numerous examples of loyalty and love between a pet owner and the pet, and I include myself in such a group of pet owners. That having been said, I now focus on one case of an older man in Westminster, MD, and his dog. The man could not be well off financially, but the dog is obviously provided for in every way. The man has no car, but he walks many blocks around town, and the dog is always at his side. The man always pushes a baby stroller to carry his belongings and possibly groceries, never a baby, but when the aging dog slows his pace, the man places the dog into the stroller and continues walking. When the man enters a store, the dog waits patiently outside for his master to return. I often thought that a photograph of this man with his dog and cart would tell the story, and no words would be necessary.

A frequent visitor to our morning coffee group at McDonald's is a friend named Paul Conaway. Just a few days ago, he told me that several months back he had actually photographed the older man and his aging dog. Then he said that in recent weeks, he once again took a picture of the man, but this time, a younger dog had replaced the older dog. We assumed that the older dog had died. Naturally, I requested copies of Paul's photos and I share them with you.

A more recent conversation with Paul Conaway revealed that the dog owner's name is apparently Joe deRita, and his older dog did die in recent months. Joe buried his loving pet in his back yard of his Westminster residence, and a white cross marks the burial spot. Joe's current dog must have been a quick replacement. Paul told Joe that photographs recently taken of Joe and his dogs could appear in my new memoir book, and this gave Joe great pleasure.

In the photo on the left, the older dog has been placed in the baby stroller by the owner. On the right, a new and younger dog is shown, and many observe that the new dog has a similar appearance to that of the old dog. Should the opportunity occur, I will engage the man in conversation if I see him walking on the streets of Westminster, but for now, I'll assume that a picture does equal a thousand words. Yes, in my opinion, a memoir can be a short story, or a poem, or even a photograph.

LIONEL LEE'S SELECTION OF A COLLEGE IN 1948

In sharp contrast to my selection of a college which was a mere 30 miles away from my Frederick home, my college classmate, Lionel Lee, sent me the following memoir, and his detailed account of his transition to Western Maryland College from a mission school in India is a story worth reading again and again. I now reproduce his story exactly as Lionel submitted it to me.

"I shall probably not make it to the 55th reunion of our class in April 2007 as it conflicts in time with my 50th reunion of my Hopkins medical school class. However I would like to contribute to the Memoir Booklet.

"My college years are among my fondest memories. I chose a scholarship to Western Maryland College over one to Asbury College in the Midwest because it was near Johns Hopkins. I had hoped to be admitted to Hopkins and thought graduation from a nearby college would boost my chances.

"In September 1948 the student population of WMC was about 700, with about 200 being from our class. The friendly atmosphere of the campus where everyone you met said "Hi" was very welcome. I was 19 years old, a graduate of Woodstock School, a mission school in the Himalayas in India. I was a World War II refugee from Singapore. When I graduated, John Dorsey, a Hostel master who was also a WMC graduate, obtained a scholarship to WMC for me. His father Lloyd was my sponsor.

"I found myself rooming with three freshmen on the fourth floor of Albert Norman Ward Hall. The dormitory was named after the third President of WMC, as was a Memorial Arch since he died during 25 years in office. My roommates, Roger Ault, Maynard Fones, Marvin Siegel, Jack Rall, Karl Yount, and Ed Earley helped me to adjust to the American culture. The language was full of slang, so that while I was speaking the same language, I often failed to understand what was being said. The Dictionary of American Slang became a frequent reference. The roommates also helped me appreciate their music collections of country western and Dixieland Jazz.

"I was one of a few foreign nationals. There were no black students. I liked Beverly Omori, a Japanese American student. I soon discovered freshmen women had to be in their dormitories at 7 p.m. Beverly transferred to the University of Southern California the following year. We remain friends to this day.

"The path to the dining hall went by the tennis courts. In winter, the fierce cold winds from the Blue Ridge Mountains of the Appalachian chain chilled our bones and almost plastered me against the tennis court fences. One sat at the same table for meals. Dress for meals was casual except at dinner when the men had to wear ties and coats and the women had to wear dresses. I learned to eat new foods. Salads, particularly the raw greens are not eaten in the Far East because vegetables then were often grown with human manure, and large portions of meat were seldom served in homes. Among the foods introduced were Maryland fried chicken, mashed potatoes, succotash, sauerkraut, Pennsylvania scrapple, apple butter, buckwheat pancakes, and Maryland crab cakes. Many are among my favorites.

"I joined a campus fraternity, Gamma Beta Chi. It had a lot of athletes among its members and had a reputation for beer drinking. Sid Albrittain, a football player, was the acknowledged chug-a lug champion. The new members, among whom was Ira Zepp, now an emeritus professor of Theology, had a bad experience with the week of hazing. We managed to change that week from Haze week to Help week. We also had a group that drank no beer, labeled by some as Coke-aholics.

"I obtained the Dean's approval for carrying a heavier credit load each semester since I was a good student. I had majors in Pre-Medical and Biology and a minor in Chemistry. I graduated with a Bachelor of Science Summa cum laude. Arrogantly, I assumed I would easily gain admission to Johns Hopkins medical school and was upset when my counselor, Dr. John Makosky, who was also Dean of Men, and the father of Donald, a classmate, suggested that I also apply to the University of Maryland. He explained that many students with just as good academic records, but with influential families, would also be applying to Hopkins, which took only 75 in its first year class. The University of Maryland took 200. He said 'You are a nobody with no money.'

"It turned out that I was the only member of my class at Hopkins that was interviewed twice by the Admissions Committee. It was interested in the fact that I had no visible financial means to attend the school. There were no grants or loans, or scholarships at that time. Dean Carmichael Tilghman later told me I was one of 75 chosen from 4200 applicants. Our class is now down to 57 because of recent deaths. After I was accepted, the staff helped me. Dr. William W. Scott, Professor of Urology, got me a job helping him with his studies on the prostate. I also worked in Emergency Chemistries and Emergency Blood Bank. My sponsor, Lloyd Dorsey, was a high school classmate of Dr. Alan Chesney. They set up a fund to help me with my tuition. Lloyd, his brother Frank, and Lloyd's friends at the Baltimore Chamber of Commerce contributed to it. I graduated from Hopkins with no debt.

"At WMC, I was a Biology major, and Dr. Harwell P. Sturdivant, the Professor, asked me to be an assistant to Freshmen Biology. I soon discovered my knowledge was superficial and I often had to admit I did not know the answer and would return later with the answers. Dr. Sturdivant was studying the large cells of the Amphiuma and asked me to help him. He came to WMC from Mississippi. He said his grandfather was devastated to learn he was going north to teach in Yankee country. He was a wonderful Southern gentleman.

"Dr. Lowell S Ensor, the 5th WMC President, came to office in 1946, the year before we arrived. I remember him as being very kind and very dignified. We often heard him at Sunday evening services, a requirement at the then Methodist College. Only two unauthorized absences per year were permitted, and it was said that students were often paid to sit in seats of students who already had two unauthorized absences. I don't know if there was any penalty for having more than two absences."

WAS MARSHA GREEN A NATIONAL THREAT?

Marsha's response to my request for a memoir was in the form of a poem, and her interesting experience does not parallel my memoirs of flight happenings. Her poem follows.

Coming Home from Houston by Green, M.B.

Like many women with more past than future
I enjoy the fruits of my years.
Married to a man of impeccable integrity,
raised two children through laughter and tears
and none of us have ever been in trouble with any of the authorities,
I tend to feel we've been a credit, not a threat to society!
We've paid our bills and taxes, recycle and always vote,
shared with the unfortunate, lived lives of quiet propriety.
No guns are allowed, no bombs or mean things
though I do admit at times I have been violent a bit
but only when flies or fleas try to invade—they do get hit!
So you might say it came as a big "downer"
coming from Houston to home
when the x-ray machine found my new manicure scissors
and enabled the inspector through my cosmetic bag to roam.
They were considered a possible threat held by possible terrorist me
that I could somehow use four-inch them to maim many and bring down the plane.
It chastens my pride to think I forgot,
I knew the rule was in effect,
but it hurts even more they are on the list
as "confiscated" and I have to return to the store!
I'm sure the three men, the x-rayer,
the prober, and boss, the one who
ruled "give them a toss,"
slept well having saved the country from me

but I'm left sleepless knowing
my government thinks I'm capable
of harming more than a flea!

MY SON-IN-LAW'S LOVE FOR OLD CARS:

My daughter met her future husband, Rob Reynolds, while both attended Gettysburg College in Gettysburg, PA. After their marriage, Rob attended graduate school to achieve his PhD, and he then accepted a teaching position at Kutztown University. Jennette devoted her time to employment as a travel agent, and, on occasion, my wife and I were able to join her on world travels. When Rob learned of my second memoir book, titled, *Family Cars Trigger Memoirs,* he responded by writing the following account of his love for old cars.

Passing on a Love for Old Cars
by Rob Reynolds

"The first old car project I recall was a 1928 Model, a two door sedan basket case my father bought in 1968when I was five years old. The previous owner took the car all apart and the failed project was secured for $250 from an ad in a local paper. The various rusted and mostly disassembled parts arrived over the course of two weekends with some parts actually toted in peach baskets. From my youthful viewpoint this seemed a monumental project. In turning a pile of rusted junk into a running car my father rose in stature before my eyes and infected me with the car collecting disease that accounts for the five collector cars and two daily drivers in my current stable of interesting vehicles, an environment that will, without a doubt, infect my young daughter with the same terminal affliction for the historic American automobile.

"The Model A project began as a partnership with dad and his brother Kip, but with the car at dad's one car garage it seemed to me that most of the work got done at our home. I remember dusting off parts of the frame and body with my Wisk broom, painting chassis parts with a paintbrush dipped in water, and mostly bearing witness to dad's diligent mission. Dad and Kip, my mom and Aunt Bobbie and the five cousins spent weekends together periodically with the five men heading off to flea markets after the regular Saturday morning big breakfast looking for car parts.

"Old cars were not a new passion for my father. He owned a variety of cars before marriage including a 1941 Chevrolet coupe and a 1937 Packard formal sedan. The Packard cost $35 when Dad bought it and is worth $50-60,000 now. For the princely sum of $350 dad bought a 1950 dechromed Mercury with frenched headlights, lowered two inches, Hollywood mufflers, and freshly machined engine parts. As a High School gear head he adopted the moniker "the spider" and made cash detailing and cosmetically repairing the cars of friends and neighbors in suburban Connecticut. Dad's greatest car experience had to be racing a 1928 Mercedes SSK down the Merritt Parkway against a second identical car that were both owned by a neighbor and were originally owned by the son of Sir Arthur Conan Doyle, the author of Sherlock Holmes. These were real race cars with drilled frames to reduce weight, supercharged engines, and dual spares on the back. I never tire of hearing how he could have bought the car for $1,500. The car is worth well over one million dollars today. That was the one that should never have gotten away.

"Dad got the Model A running. He did most of the work himself including the painting and interior work and for a few years we tooled around town on joy rides with the family. The car made the local paper about 1970 as part of a demonstration in support of teachers. When my uncle got a turn with the car he brought it home and traded it for a 1928 Buick. The Buick had wood spoke wheels and a nice blue body and it spent part of a year in dad's garage before going back to my uncle, and turning into another trade that never returned to dad.

"By the time I was ten my dad no longer had the money or time for old cars. My interest in old cars was then nurtured by my Uncle Kip who turned the Model A into a 1928 Buick, then into a 1937 Buick, then a 1940 Ford convertible kept company by a 1929 Model A Ford roadster with a rumble seat, a 1947 Ford woody station wagon a 1947 Ford pickup and a few 1970s end of the line convertibles. I think there was a Kennedy era Lincoln Continental convertible mixed into the lot as well. Each time we visited my uncle and his family part of the ritual was heading out to the garage to see the old cars and take at least one out for a joy ride. My cousins and I often snuck out to the garage to play in the cars and pretend to explore the great American landscape in these antique machines.

"About the time dad got away from old cars he bought a new car that I really liked. The new maroon with black interior 1973 firebird turned out to be a key link in my evolving interest in old cars. The firebird was a lot cooler than the traded in 1968 VW bug that had its windshield shot out during the Newark riots and was rear ended at five miles per hour and was nearly totaled. The firebird was the base model with a 350 cubic inch engine, two barrel carburetor, automatic transmission, and single exhaust. It had white wall tires, wheel covers, an am radio and one real luxury item; air-conditioning. While the firebird certainly had limited power and performance it was an awesome color and it was a pony car and part of the muscle car phenomenon. Pontiac excitement hit my family hard with mom buying a 1974 Grand Prix and a Grand Safari Wagon around 1980.

"A few months before earning my New Jersey driver's license dad decided it was time to replace the firebird with a 1979 Firebird Formula. His timing was perfect. I had some money saved up and he sold me the six year old firebird for about $800. It was rusting around the sides of the rear window and in the panels behind and in front of the rear wheels, but the cancer was pretty minimal and many years of care and polishing left the maroon paint with a high gloss. On the day I passed my driver's test I headed off to Newark with a family friend to a car stereo discounter and bought an am/fm cassette player, front speakers for the doors, and large 6" x 9" coaxial speakers for the rear package shelf. My friend helped install the stereo and the transformation of dad's firebird into Rob's firebird had begun.

"I started working at gas stations during school and at our summer place during summer vacation. I made friends with mechanics and got advice and help with the Firebird. On my way to my summer job I had to pull far over on a narrow road to avoid an oil truck and I bent two rims and punctured two tires. When I called work they sent the wrecker for the firebird. It just so happened that one of the mechanics had four slotted mag wheels that fit the firebird. I picked up four new BF Goodrich Radial TAs and the car never handled so well. To keep the big rear tires from rubbing I added air shocks and adjusted the rake of the car to a more menacing angle. Yellow traction bars bolted to the rear leaf springs reduced wheel hop when burning rubber from a dead stop. In less than a year I had to replace the brakes and the transmission had to be rebuilt.

"As a junior in high school pumping gas I met up with another mechanic who prescribed a number of changes to the firebird. He convinced me to upgrade the engine with dual exhaust, an Edelbrock manifold, a 650 Holley carburetor, hotter Accel wires and a better race tuned engine. To handle better we ordered the year appropriate Trans Am handling package that included stiffer front springs, a thicker front sway bar and a rear sway bar. The firebird became much more of a street racing machine that could handle. I was in car heaven.

"After four years of college and starting my first real job working as an apprentice for the National Trust for Historic Preservation I started yearning for a new car. I looked at the third generation Firebird Trans Am but decided instead to buy a Fiero. I liked the Fiero because it was made of enduroflex and would not rust. It was a rear engine car, handled well, and as a two passenger car it seemed perfect for me as a 22 year old. I wanted the GT model, but they were not available due to retooling for a redesign so I ordered the SE model with many of the options found on the GT. I ordered the high output V-6 engine, a four speed, a hot stereo with cassette, and the removable sun roof. I sadly sold the 1973 Firebird to my uncle's youngest son Carl who took it to Paris Island when he joined the Marines and later sold it to someone in Virginia. I still check eBay Firebirds for sale each week and have yet to see the car I let go of that I still regret selling.

"When my grandmother passed away Dad got back into old cars buying a 1928 Model A Ford roadster, a 1938 Ford convertible sedan with the distinctive early V-8, a 1946 Mercury convertible, and finally a 1929 Model A speedster that evoked the SSK from his youth. The speedster had a hopped up engine, a Lincoln clutch, a special open body and had sat for twenty years unfinished. Dad almost sent it back after looking over the project after delivery, but he broke the project into parts and took each one on systematically until he was done.

"I knew I wanted old cars in my life, but my income as a perpetual graduate student limited my options. I did turn up a somewhat worn out 1949 Plymouth Special Deluxe that I purchased from the owner's father-in-law who signed the car over to me in return for reimbursing him for the four new tires he purchased as a Christmas present. The son-in-law had just run away with another woman. I keep trying to sell the Plymouth, but my daughter cries when I talk about it and my wife gets mad and tells me it is the car she like the most in the garage. Now it is a fixture at the local garage where it is slowly being made road worthy for the first time in fifteen years. Maybe I will drive her to work in the spring.

"Then there is the Model T project. I fell in love with the idea of having a primitive early car. Without ever trying to drive a T, I decided to restore one. A suitable basket case was found in a pole barn in Connecticut and my dad and I managed to fit all the parts into my old Ford F-150. Dad had just retired and was willing to put the car in his garage and take on most of the labor. Armed with my credit card and researching skills dad spent over a year bringing the Model T back to life. Of all the things my father ever did for me, restoring the Model T was the most precious gift of all for it symbolized the renewal of a bond over cars that we have shared since I can remember. When we hauled the Model T out to Indiana for the Model T Centennial we won second place in our class, a feat dad was so proud to recount to all our car friends.

"The Model T has not traveled many miles. It turns out that being 6'-2" makes it hard to operate the pedals and the car's planetary transmission is a bit scary to operate. While I really like keeping the car in great condition I lacked the confidence to really enjoy driving the car. That bittersweet emotion led me to think more and more about the old 1973 Firebird.

"For several years I followed firebird auctions on eBay and I occasionally took a look at local cars for sale. Inevitably, most had major problems, were hot rodded, rusted, poorly repaired, and beyond my skill level to set right. Not long after receiving tenure at Kutztown University I found the car I was looking for. I located an expired auction for a 1971 Firebird Formula. The car had 46,000 miles; the 400 engine with a Hurst shifted four speed, and factory rally II wheels. I called the owner and found out it was still for sale. We struck a deal on a leap of faith and a dozen and a half photographs. The car was in Minnesota and I live in Pennsylvania. I sent a bank check, waited for it to clear, sent a transport company to get the car, waited a week, and took delivery. The car was pretty much as described but did have some issues that were not fully disclosed. However, the rarity and value of the car left me feeling I still made a good deal. Sitting in my new Firebird is akin to entering a time machine that makes me sixteen years old again with all the hope, naiveté, and sense of everything still being possible. Anytime I feel stressed or down I can transform myself by shifting through the gears of my Muncie transmission chirping the tires with each shift.

"When working in the garage among the Firebird, Fiero, Plymouth, Model T, and a late model Chrysler Sebring Convertible now in preservation my eight year old daughter often visits. She climbs into each car, pretends to drive, and tells me why one car in particular is her current favorite. She helps me wash and vacuum the cars and sometimes she accompanies me to car shows. In her actions I see myself as a child falling in love with cars as an extension of my love for my dad, uncle, and cousins. I have to wonder which of the cars in my collection she will take on and care for in memory of our relationship and love of great American automobiles. In eight years Reanna will get her license. What will she drive as a first car? I am already scouting for a first generation Firebird 400 convertible to "loan" her for high school. I can't wait to see her behind the wheel of her own muscle car like the old man, and his old man."

A 1953 English film named *Genevieve*

As I reflect on my son-in-law's numerous experiences with his old cars, I am reminded of the award-winning 1953 English film called *Genevieve*. This film was a pleasure to me when I first viewed it some 50+ years ago, and recent showings on TV have been equally enjoyable. The two movie leads were John Gregson and Dinah Sheridan, but those in the minor roles, Kenneth More and Kay Kendall, are the two stars I most remember.

The story is about the annual veteran car run between London and Brighton, and John and Ken in the film own 1904 cars. They complete the run to Brighton, but then in an aroused state, they bet on the return to London, making it a race to the Westminster Bridge. Ken's underhanded tactics seems to be determining the outcome of the race, but at the last second, Ken's car is diverted from the bridge by getting the car's wheels caught in tram lines, forcing the car to turn away from the Bridge and possible victory. The film is great fun, and I heartily recommend it to all lovers of old cars.

MY BROTHER RECALLED HIS FIRST PLANE FLIGHT

My only living brother is Dr. Charles Shook, a former Methodist minister who now resides in Anna Maria, Florida. Charlie was born in 1928 and my birth was in 1930. He hardly ever answers my phone calls, and my messages left on his phone record that his much younger brother has called once again without success. The one time he did answer his phone, I concluded that he must have failed to look at the caller ID window. On that occasion, we did discuss my two memoir books, *Getting Hooked on Memoirs* and *Family Cars Trigger Memoirs*, and I believe my memoirs did shake the dust off of some of his past memories.

Charlie claims that he wrote a response to my two books, but that the computer lost the material or perhaps the dog ate the papers. Come to think of it, he does not have a dog. Well, nevertheless, I'll share what he said verbally over the phone. When I revealed that our step-brother, Herman, taught me to drive his Nash coop in 1946, Charlie responded that our father taught him to drive in 1944. I believe Charlie has this correct, because Herman was stationed in England in 1944, and he later returned home with an English war-bride. My memoir about my first plane flight in 1957 does not resemble Charlie's plane experience. In my case, I was soon to be discharged from the military, and I used my 46-day leave to visit Europe. Wearing my uniform to the McGuire Air Force Base in New Jersey, I was able to receive a free flight to Europe, stopping in the Azores to refuel on the 17 hour flight across the Atlantic Ocean. The photo on the next page shows my view from the plane's window on that first flight. Looking down on the clouds beneath the plane, I thought it would be great fun to jump up and down on this cotton-like bed of clouds.

Charlie's first flight was actually a round trip passage between Boston and Baltimore, and I doubt that it had four propellers as did my plane. He had been requested to return to his former Maryland church to perform a memorial service, and his schedule would not allow him to drive the lengthy round trip. Rather than accept his regrets, the family requesting his services offered to cover the costs of a round-trip flight. Charlie's thoughts about the memorial service gave little time for him to enjoy the flight to Baltimore, but he was able to fully enjoy the return flight to Boston. While looking out the plane's window at the clouds below, he was tapped on the head by someone walking through the plane. To Charlie's surprise, he was struck on the head by a former college classmate, and this fellow was one of the pilots on that particular flight.

The pilot, Al Lovelace, who had shared many fun moments with Charlie on the Western Maryland College campus, invited Charlie to join him in the front cabin. This became a very unique experience for Charlie, especially considering it was part of his first flight experience. As the plane circled Boston for the opportunity to land, the pilot may have disregarded flight rules, because he allowed Charlie to remain in the cockpit for the landing. They came in low over the water on the approach to the runway, and Charlie thought the wheels might strike the water. When Charlie opened his eyes, he realized that the plane had made a safe landing and that he was once again on the ground. His college classmate had made it an experience that Charlie will always remember.

A 1970 WMC Faculty Club's Book of Recipes:

On October 31, 1970, I was serving a term as President of the Western Maryland College (WMC) Faculty Club. As a club project, favorite recipes were collected and printed as a booklet for distribution. Booklets were given to club members at a pot-luck dinner, and the 1970 *Faculty Club Recipe Book* became a prized possession. At the pot-luck dinner, families could sample the foods that matched the collected recipes, and no members departed early that evening. Club meetings always concluded with desserts and beverages, and a number of pot-luck dinners were also scheduled each year. In the 1960s and early 1970s, the Faculty Club meetings were popular events, and those attending would fill the meeting area, namely McDaniel Lounge of the college. Families of faculty and staff would take advantage of these opportunities to socialize with other members of the college family, and attendance at meetings ranged from 40 to 80, pot-luck dinners drawing the largest crowds. Guest speakers were often invited to discuss a variety of current topics, and musical entertainment was not overlooked. A faculty quartet (Griswold, Holthaus, Shook, & Spangler) was even known to perform on occasion.

On the pages that follow, I will attempt to provide the reader with most of the recipes found in the original *Faculty Club Recipe Book* printed in 1970. The first printing was 7" by 8 ½" in size and was 30 pages in length. At least one copy of the original booklet has been placed in the Western Maryland College Archives. I know that these recipes have not lost their value over the past 39 years, and I will mention just a few at this point. Mrs. Lowell Ensor, President Ensor's wife, shared her recipe for "Baked Limas with Sour Cream," and Mrs. Harwell Sturdivant listed her "Pudding Cake." Florence Earp shared her "Pumpkin Pie," and Registrar Martha Manahan revealed her secrets in making prize-winning "Mints." Mrs. Theodore Whitfield's recipe was for "Hamburger Sour Cream Casserole," and Sheila Buttner guided the reader in the preparation of "Swedish Meatballs."

Special thanks must be given to my wife, Carol, and to Mr. and Mrs. Alex Ober for their work on the original 1970 *Faculty Club Recipe Book*. Much time was required to collect recipes and to organize the book's contents.

THE 1970 WMC FACULTY CLUB RECIPE BOOK

MAIN DISHES:

Escobeche de Gallina (Peru)—Cold Pickled Chicken

Use: 1/3 cup olive oil ; 6-8 pieces of chicken (cut up) ; 1 c. dry white wine; 1 c. distilled white vinegar; 1 c. hot water; 2 medium onions (peeled, halved, & in wedges); 3 carrots (scraped & cut diagonally); ; 1 small leek (I used green onion) cut into rounds; 1 T salt; 1 bouquet of celery tops; 2 parsley sprigs, 2 bay leaves; 2 whole cloves, and ¼ tsp. thyme wrapped together in cheesecloth; 1 lemon (cut lengthwise into halves and crosswise into thin slices); * I added ½ tbsp. gelatin

In heavy 4-5 qt. casserole heat the olive oil—don't let oil smoke. Put in chicken (I skinned mine) and brown in oil—turn with tongs. Add wine, vinegar, water, onions, carrots, leek, salt, and bouquet and bring to boil over high heat. Reduce heat to low, cover casserole and simmer undisturbed for 30 minutes. Chicken should be tender, but not falling off the bone.

Remove bouquet and arrange chicken pieces in serving dish just large enough to hold snugly in one layer. (At this point I add gelatin to the cooling liquid.) Pour cooking liquid and vegetables over chicken. Decorate top with lemon slices. Cool and then refrigerate at least six hours.

⌐∿⌐

Beef Casserole, Chinese Style—Ethel O. deLong

1 lb ground round; 2 T cream; 1 pkg frozen peas (thawed) ; 1 ½ t salt; 2 c (finely sliced raw celery) ; ½ t pepper; 1 can (10 oz) mushroom soup; 1 small onion (finely chopped); 1 c crushed potato chips

Brown beef in fry pan until brown and crumbly, adding fat if necessary; turn into 1 ½ quart casserole. Arrange thawed peas over browned meat, then cover with sliced celery. Mix together the mushroom soup, cream, salt, pepper, and onion; pour over celery. Sprinkle potato chips over top of casserole. Bake at 375 degrees for 30 min. or until hot and bubbly. Do not overcook. Serves 6. Can be prepared in individual casseroles (cut baking time to 20 minutes).

⌐∿⌐

Eggplant Parmesan—Recipe of Ethel O. deLong

1 large eggplant; 3 eggs (beaten); 1 c packaged dry bread crumbs; ¾ c olive or salad oil

Pare eggplant if desired; cut in ¼" slices. Dip each slice in eggs, then crumbs. Sauté in hot oil in skillet until golden on both sides. Layer in two quart casserole with: ½ c grated Parmesan, ½ lb. grated Mozzarella, 2 ts dried oregano, 3 8oz. cans tomato sauce. Cover well with tomato sauce, topping last layer with Mozarella. Bake uncovered ½ hour or until sauce is bubbly and cheese is melted.

⌐∿⌐

Elizabeth's Chicken Noodle Casserole From Ruth Ann Stevens

2 pk. frozen broccoli ; 4 cups cooked chicken (or ham or ½ each) ; 2 cans cream of chicken soup (undiluted) ; 1 cup mayonnaise;

juice of 1 lemon; 1 teaspoon curry powder; 2 cups shredded sharp cheddar cheese; 2 3 oz. cans chow mien noodles

Cook the broccoli & drain, arrange in a greased baking dish. Place the meat on top, cut to bite-size chunks. Mix the soup, mayonnaise, lemon juice & curry powder together & pour over the meat. Sprinkle with cheese. Put noodles on top & bake in 350 degree oven for 30 minutes. This dish can be fixed the day before and kept in refrigerator. Allow a little extra heating time in this case.

Chicken Noodles—Use: 2 cut-up 3 lb. chickens; 3 quarts water; 2 tbsp. salt; 2 cups cut-up carrots; 2 thinly sliced medium sized onions; 2 tbsp. dried parsley; 1 12 oz. bag square egg noodles; 1 quart water ; ½ cup flour; ½ cup milk ; ½ tsp. pepper; ½ cup butter

In large sauce pan add chicken, water, & salt. Cook until chicken is tender. Remove chicken from broth, bone & cut-up. Strain broth. Cook carrots, onions, and parsley in 2 cups broth. Return remaining broth plus 1 quart water to heat and bring to rolling boil. Add noodles (2 or 3 at a time) & cook until tender, stirring occasionally. Add carrots, onions, parsley, & broth (cooked in) to noodles. Blend flour and milk and add to noodle mixture (stir until thickened). Add butter, pepper, and cut-up chicken. (Serves 10-12).

~m~

Crab Casserole (Serves 4-6)—From Mary Lee Schmall

2 cups thick white sauce; 1 can mushroom soup (undiluted); 1 pkg 8 oz. pasteurized American cheese (melt in sauce and soup); add green pepper & 1 lb. crab meat; season to taste with garlic salt & pepper; Bake at 350 degrees for ¾ hour.

~m~

Baked Beans—(New England)—From Jean Zauche

Rinse and soak a pound of navy beans overnight. In the morning, rinse, cover with water, add ¼ pound salt pork, bring to a boil and then simmer until beans pop open and are a little soft.

Put in baking dish and add 3 tbsp. each of white granulated sugar and light molasses, 1 tsp. salt, and 1 small onion. Mix well. Bake for around 3 hours at 350 degrees, uncovered, and add just enough water to cover beans.

⁓

Swedish Meatballs—Sheila Buttner Recipe

Mix 1 lb. ground beef & ½ lb. ground pork (extra beef could be substituted for pork); ½ cup minced onions & ¼ cup bread crumbs; 1 tbsp. parsley, 1 ½ tsp. salt, & 1/8 tsp. pepper; 1 tsp. Worcestershire sauce & 1 egg; 4 slices of bread or rolls (softened in water and squeezed out); ¼ cup milk & shape into size of walnuts.

Brown in ½ cup fat or vegetable oil; remove meatballs and make gravy. Stir in pan: ¼ cup flour, 1 tsp. paprika, ½ tsp. salt, & 1 1/8 tsp. pepper. Add 2 cups boiling water & ¾ cup sour cream. Return meatballs to gravy for at least twenty minutes and simmer slowly.

⁓

Seafood Casserole—From Mrs. Theodore Whitfield

½ cup minced onion & ½ minced green pepper; 4 tbsp. margarine (melted); 1 10-oz. can cream of mushroom soup; 1 2-oz. can chopped mushrooms & liquid; 1 cup milk & 3 cups of cooked rice; 1 lb. cooked shrimp; 1 6 1/2-oz. can king crab meat, flaked; ¾ cup cheddar cheese, grated; 1 cup soft buttered bread crumbs

Sauté onion and pepper in margarine. Combine soup, mushrooms, and milk; simmer with onion and pepper for ten minutes. Add rice. Cut shrimp in halves; add with crab to rice mixture. Place in 2-quart casserole. Sprinkle top with cheese and bread crumbs. Bake at 350 degrees for 45 minutes. (Makes 6-8 servings).

↶ฦ↷

Hamburger Sour Cream Casserole—Mrs. Whitfield

1 lb. hamburger & 1 tbsp. butter; 2 8-oz. cans tomato sauce; 1 cup cottage cheese & ¼ cup sour cream; 1 tbsp. onion flakes; 1 tbsp. chopped green peppers; 1 cup macaroni (fine); could add 8 oz. cream cheese (if desired).

Cook macaroni and drain. Skillet brown the meat in butter. Pour off excess fat and stir in tomato sauce. Remove from heat. Combine cheese, sour cream, onion and pepper. In a buttered two qt. casserole, put ½ of the macaroni, then the cheese mixture and the rest of the macaroni. Cover with meat on top and bake in 350 degree oven for 30 minutes.

↶ฦ↷

Stuffed Beef Round—Mildred Cole (Mrs. Gerald Cole)

Use: 2 lb. beef round steak (cut ½" thick); 4 oz. sharp cheese (shredded); ½ cup chopped onions; ½ cup chopped celery; ¼ cup snipped parsley; ¼ cup all-purpose flour; tsp. salt; 1/8 tsp. pepper; 2 tbsp. cooking oil; 1 10 ½ oz. can condensed beef broth; ½ tsp. dry mustard; 2 tbsp. all-purpose flour; ¼ cup water

Cut steak into 6 serving-size pieces; pound to ¼ inch thickness. Combine: cheese, onion, celery, and parsley. Place about ¼ cup cheese mixture in center of each piece of steak, reserving remainder cheese mixture (about 1 cup). Roll up each steak jelly-roll fashion; secure with wooden picks. Combine the ¼ cup of flour, the salt, and the pepper. Roll meat in the flour mixture to coat. In skillet, slowly brown meat in hot oil. Drain off excess fat. Combine beef broth and mustard; add to steak rolls. Cover and simmer 45 minutes. Add reserved cheese mixture to skillet; simmer 15 to 30 minutes more or until meat is tender. Remove meat to heated platter. Skim excess fat from pan juices. Blend together the 2 tbsp. flour and the water; stir into the pan juices. Cook, stirring constantly, til sauce thickens and bubbles; pour over meat rolls. (Makes 6 servings)

~M~

Stuffed Green Peppers (Mashed potatoes & ground beef)

Use: **4-6 green peppers; 1 lb. ground chuck; 1 1 ½ oz. pkg. dehydrated onion soup; mashed (or instant) potatoes**

Wash peppers and remove seeds. Parboil in boiling water, 2-3 minutes. Combine beef and onion soup; brown meat in skillet (over low heat). Remove from heat; add to whipped potatoes. Stuff peppers with meat-potato mixture. Place in mixing dish. Bake at 350 degrees for 45-50 minutes or until tender. Serve with favorite tomato sauce. Hint: Start Ground beef first; then add onion soup mix. Cool beef before mixing with potatoes.

~M~

Poulet Farigoule (Chicken cooked in white wine) Recipe is from Provence, France and Mrs. Jacqueline DeRasse.

Use: **1 3 lb. chicken; 1 tbsp. olive oil; 1 tbsp. (1/2 oz.) butter; chopped parsley; 2 or 3 cloves of garlic, chopped; flour; 1 cup (UK scant ½ pint) bouillon; 1 cup (UK scant ½ pint) dry white wine; 8 oz. mushrooms; 4 medium tomatoes; 5 oz. green olives, stoned; sprig each of rosemary, thyme and fennel.**

Cut up the uncooked chicken meat in butter. Heat the olive oil and butter in a heavy skillet and add the pieces of chicken, cooking them to a golden color. When they are about half-browned, sprinkle with the chopped parsley and garlic. When brown, add a little flour, cook the chicken until done, then add the bouillon and white wine. Simmer for one hour. Wash and slice the mushrooms and add to the chicken, along with the tomatoes, which have been quartered and the stoned olives. Add the rosemary, fennel and thyme. Simmer 30 minutes longer. (Serves 4) Preparation time: 20 minutes Cooking time: 2 hours

SALADS AND VEGETABLES:

Twenty-Four Hour Salad

Use: 1 egg; 2 tbsp. fresh, frozen, or canned lemon juice; 2 tbsp. sugar; pinch of salt; ½ cup heavy cream, whipped, or 1 pkg. dream whip as mixed on box; 1 cup miniature marshmallows; 4 cups fruit (1 large can of fruit cocktail); 1 can pineapple chunks (well drained); 2 cans mandarin oranges

In double boiler, beat egg well. Add lemon juice, sugar, salt, and cook til thickened. Remove from heat and add marshmallows. Cool. Pour over fruit and mix well. Add whipped cream. Refrigerate for 24 hours.

cm

Cranberry-Chicken Mold—From Julia T. Hitchcock

Bottom Layer (Cranberry Orange)—Grind together: 2 c. raw cranberries & 2 oranges; mix with ¾ c. sugar; set 1 hour. Add ½ c. chopped nuts. Mix with 1 pack red jello made with 1 ½ c. water. Fill bottom half of mold & set in refrigerator until jelled.

Top Layer (Chicken)—Use 1 envelope unflavored gelatin, softened in ¼ cup water. Dissolve in 1 ¼ c. hot chicken broth. Then add: ¾ c. mayonnaise, 1 T. lemon juice, 2 c. cooked chicken (chopped), salt, 1 c. finely cut celery; salt & pepper.

Cover molded cranberry mixture, and set in refrigerator until jelled. May be served with cottage cheese and garnished with parsley. (Serves 12)

⌒⁘⌒

<u>Mandarin Duet Salad</u>—From Annie Laurie Clark

Use: 2-3 oz. pkg. orange jello; 2 c. boiling water or fruit juice; 1 pt. orange sherbet; 1 11oz. can mandarin oranges, drained; add Ambrosia Fruit Salad

Dissolve gelatin in boiling liquid. Add sherbet, stirring until melted. Add orange; pour into 1 ½ qt. ring mold. Chill until firm. Unmold; fill center with Ambrosia Salad.

Ambrosia Fruit Salad—Use: 1 11oz. can mandarin oranges (drained); 1 13oz. can pineapple chunks (drained); 1 c. flaked coconut; 1 c. of miniature marshmallows; ½ c. sour cream or ½ c. whipped cream

Combine all ingredients. Chill for 5 hours or overnight. Serves 10-12.

⌒⁘⌒

<u>Potato Salad</u>—Bernice Beard Recipe

1 egg ; 1 tbsp. corn starch; 1 cup sugar; 1 ½ tsp. dry mustard, or prepared mustard; ¼ cup vinegar, or slightly less; ¾ cup water

Beat egg slightly. Add cornstarch, sugar, dry mustard and mix in water and vinegar (or combine in blender for 25 seconds on "Whip"). Bring to boil in 1 ½ qt. saucepan. If high heat is used, stir to keep from sticking and getting lumpy. When mixture reaches a full rolling boil, set aside to cool. When cool, blend in, using a tablespoon, about 1 cup of salad dressing, prepared, like Mrs. Filbert's. Mixture will be a little lumpy when salad dressing is mixed in. Combine with potato Mixture (below). Garnish with slices of hard—boiled egg sprinkled with paprika.

Potato Mixture—Use: 10 medium to small potatoes; 1 cup celery, chopped; ¼ cup onion, chopped or 1 tsp. dried minced onion reconstituted; 1 tsp. celery salt; 4 hard-boiled eggs

Peel potatoes. Boil with 1 tsp. salt until done. Set aside to cool. To hard-boil the eggs, place 4 eggs (older eggs preferred over fresh ones for better peeling) in cold water that covers them. Put lid on pan and set on burner with high heat. When water comes to a full boil, turn off heat and let pan and eggs on burner for 20 minutes. Remove from burner, drain water, and run cold water over eggs to cool quickly. Peel. Chop three of them. Toss diced or chopped potatoes, celery, onion, celery salt, and chopped egg with fork. Mix in dressing (above). Mixture should be oozy with dressing. Makes 3 pints of potato salad. For Faculty Club, I tripled the recipe.

⌒⁂⌒

Peas And Carrots—Esther G Royer Recipe

Take 1 ½ cups sliced carrots, 1 ½ cups fresh (or frozen) peas. Cook in salt water seasoned with butter. When tender, drain off liquid. Add about ½ cup of creamed cheese sauce (or Cream of Mushroom soup). Simmer for a few minutes and serve hot.

⌒⁂⌒

Creamy Carrot-Nut Mold—Esther G. Royer Recipe

(To prepare: 30 minutes. To chill: 4-5 hours) Use: 1 6oz. pkg. orange-flavored gelatin; 2 cups very hot water; 1 cup thick sour cream; 1 13 ½ oz. can (1 & 2/3 cups) crushed pineapple (do not drain); 2 cups grated carrots & ½ cup chopped walnuts

Lightly oil a 2 qt. mold with salad or cooking oil (not olive oil); set aside to drain. Pour hot water over gelatin in a bowl and stir until the gelatin is completely dissolved. Gradually add gelatin mixture to sour cream, stirring until well blended. Chill until mixture begins to gel (becomes slightly thicker). If mixture is chilled in refrigerator, stir occasionally; if chilled over ice and water, stir frequently. Stir in pineapple, grated carrots, and chopped nuts.

Turn into the mold and chill until firm, about 4 hours. Unmold into a bed of salad greens on a chilled serving plate. Garnish with a carrot curl, walnut halves, and a border of carrot flowers. (Serves 8-10.)

⁂

Pickled Bean Salad—Mrs. Alspach Recipe

Use: 1 can waxed beans; 1 can French-style green beans; 1 can red kidney beans; ½ cup minced green pepper and/or celery; ½ cup minced onion; pimento

Mix together and marinate for 24 hours in: ½ cup vinegar, ¾ cup white sugar, ½ cup salad oil, 1 tsp. salt, 1 tsp. pepper.

⁂

Jellied Beet Salad—Mrs. Alspach Recipe

Put I pkg. lemon-flavored jello and 1 cup hot beet juice (juice from 1 lb. can and water) in blender. Cover and blend on high speed 20 seconds. Add 1 ½ to 2 tsp. lemon juice, 1 tsp. salt, ½ very small onion, 1 tbsp. horseradish, and 1 lb. cooked beets. Cover and blend on high speed 10 seconds or until beets are coarsely chopped. Pour into 3-4 cup molds and chill until time to serve. Serve with sour cream.

⁂

Raspberry Apple Salad—Marjorie Spangler Recipe

Use: 1 pkg. raspberry Jello; 1 whole unpeeled apple; 1 can crushed pineapple (small 3/4 cup); ½ cup chopped nuts

Add ½ cup boiling water to Jello. Stir until dissolved. Add ¾ cup cold orange juice. Partially jell. Add remaining ingredients and chill until set. Serves 6.

Dressing—Mix small pkg. of cream cheese with ¼ cup powdered sugar. Add enough fruit juice to gain consistency of salad dressing.

◦◦◦

Green Jello Salad—Mary Ellen Elwell Recipe

Use: 1 large box lime Jello; ¾ cup water; 1 large can pears; 1 large block cream cheese; 1 pt. cool whip or dream whip

Dissolve Jello in boiling water and pear juice. Puree pears and cream cheese (in blender or with electric mixer). Add pears and cream cheese to hot lime mixture. Set 3 hours. Fold in Dream Whip.

◦◦◦

Baked Limas With Sour Cream—Mrs. Lowell Ensor Recipe

Use: 1 lb. dried baby lima beans; 3 tsp. salt; ¾ cup butter or margarine; ¾ cup brown sugar (firmly packed); 1 tbsp. dry mustard; 1 tbsp. molasses; 1 cup sour cream

Soak lima beans overnight. Drain and cover with fresh water. Add 1 tsp. of salt and cook until tender, about 30-40 minutes. Drain again and rinse under hot water. Put in medium casserole container. Dab butter over hot beans. Mix brown sugar, mustard and remaining salt together and sprinkle over beans. Stir in molasses, and finally sour cream, mixing gently. Bake for one hour at 350 degrees. Can be prepared ahead of time and tucked into oven an hour before serving time. Serves 8.

⌒*ᵐ*⌒

Orange Salad—Contributed by Corinne Schofield

Use: 2 3oz. pkg. (or 1 large pkg.) orange Jello; 2 cups boiling liquid (save orange juice, pineapple juice, and water); 1 pt. orange sherbet; 1 can crushed pineapple; 1 large can of mandarin oranges

Dissolve jello in boiling liquid. Add orange sherbet. Use slotted spoon and mash until all is melted. Add pineapple and orange. Pour into a mold and chill. Serves 12-14.

DESSERTS:

Bundt Cake—Contributed by Joan Tait

Use: 1 ¼ cup butter or margarine; 2 ½ cup sugar; Cream butter and sugar; 7 eggs added (unbeaten) one at a time; 2 ½ cups flour (add all at once and beat well); 2 ½ tsp. vanilla or lemon extract

Pour into greased bundt cake pan. Bake at 325 degrees for 1 hr. or till done. Cool 10 minutes before removing from pan.

⌒*ᵐ*⌒

Date Cake—Contributed by Joan Tait

Use: 1 cup chopped dates; 1 tsp. soda sprinkled over dates; 1 cup boiling water poured over dates; set to cool; 1 cup sugar & ½ cup shortening; 1 egg; 1 ½ cups flour, alternate dates and flour; ½ cup walnut meats, with a pinch of salt; 1 tsp. vanilla

Bake 30 minutes in 350 degree oven.

⌒*ᴍ*⌒

Date & Rice Krispie Cookies

Use: 1 stick margarine & 1 cup sugar; ½ lb. chopped dates & 1 egg; 1 cup nuts & coconut & Rice Krispies

Mix egg, sugar, margarine and dates, and then cook about 10 minutes or until dates are melted, stirring constantly. Pour this mixture over 2 to 3 cups of Rice Krispies and add nuts. Make into small balls and roll in coconut. Cool.

⌒*ᴍ*⌒

Saucepan Brownies

Use: 1 stick margarine & 2 1oz. sqs. of chocolate; 1 cup sugar & 1 cup nuts & ½ cup flour; 1 tsp. baking powder; 1 tsp. vanilla; 2 eggs

Rub bottom 9" sq. pan with oleo. Melt oleo & chocolate in saucepan over low heat. Add all ingredients (except eggs) to blend. Add eggs and heat well. Pour into prepared pan. Bake at 350 degrees for 30 minutes. Cool in pan.

⌒*ᴍ*⌒

Angel—Pudding Cake—Mrs. Harwell P. Sturdivant

Make up any angel food mix according to directions on box. After cake is cooled, slice it into 3 layers.

Filling and Icing: Mix and let set 2 packages instant lemon pudding mix and 2 cups of milk. Fold into about 2 cups dream whip (whipped) and spread between layers and ice entire cake. Store in refrigerator until ready to serve 12-15 guests.

Note: Any flavor of angel food mix and instant custard pudding may be used. I prefer Duncan Hines Deluxe Cake Mix and Jello instant custard mix. The cake may be baked a day ahead and iced several hours before its use. (Keeps several days in the refrigerator.)

Lime Chiffon Pie—Contributed by Day Sisk

Prepare 1 pie shell, bake & cooled.

Blend & cook over medium heat until boiling slightly. Use: 1 box lemon pie filling; 1 envelope unflavored gelatin; ½ cup sugar; 2 egg yolks; 2 ½ cups water; juice from 1 lime (or put the entire lime in blender with some of the water & puree it); 3 drops green food coloring

Cool 15 minutes. Beat, then fold into pudding, using 2 egg whites and ¼ cup sugar. (Beat until glossy)

Pour into pie shell & chill. At the last minute before serving, cover pie with whipped cream or cool whip or dream whip, etc. Garnish with lime "slivers." (Makes 1 large generously filled pie or two 8" pies.)

Tunnel of Fudge Cake—Mrs. Florence Earp

Beat 1 ½ cups soft butter at high speed until fluffy. Beat in 6 eggs (one at a time). Gradually beat in 1 ½ cups sugar. Beat until fluffy. By hand, stir in 2 cups Pillsbury's Best All Purpose Flour, dry frosting mix (Double Dutch) and 2 cups chopped walnuts until blended. Bake in greased Bundt (or 10" tube pan) at 350 degrees for 55-60 min. (until top is dry & shiny). Cool in pan for two hours.

Pumpkin Pie—Contributed by Florence Earp

Use: 1 baked 9" crust; 1 envelope gelatin-Knox; 4 tbsp. cold water; 3 eggs (separated); 1 cup brown sugar; ½ cup milk; 1 ½ cup canned pumpkin; 2 tsp. cinnamon; ½ tsp. ginger; ¼ tsp. allspice; 3 tbsp. sugar

Add water to gelatin. Combine egg yolks, sugar, milk, pumpkin, & spices in top of double boiler. Cook for 10 min. Add gelatin & cool. Add beaten egg whites and sugar. Pour into pie shell. Serve with whipped cream.

꿈

Chocolate and Almond Bavarian (Serves 8 guests)—Edith Ridington Recipe

Heat over boiling water 2 cups milk mixed with 2/3 cup sugar and a pinch of salt. When hot, add ½ cup finely ground almonds. Cover and remove from heat, allow flavors to blend for 15 minutes. Soak 4 tsp. plain gelatin in ½ cup cold milk. Add this to the above and heat until dissolved. Cool and add 1 tsp. almond flavoring. When it is beginning to thicken, beat hard until fluffy. Beat 1 cup heavy cream til stiff, and fold into above mixture. Pour into mold and chill until firm. Coat with a thick chocolate sauce.

꿈

Mints—Award Winning Recipe from WMC Registrar Martha Manahan

Blend well: 1 lb. 10x sugar, ½ stick margarine (melted), 3 tbsp. cold water, ¼ tsp. Imitation Butter Extract, 2 tsp. peppermint extract (Safeway Crown Glory), 6-8 drops of oil of peppermint, and coloring as desired.

Knead well and form into balls, pressing each ball in palm of the hand and place on waxed paper. Imprint design with butter press.

Place in airtight container and keep in refrigerator. If fondant is too soft, add more sugar—if too stiff, add a drop or more of water.

ﾘ

Strawberry Jam Cake—Arleen Heggemeier Recipe

Use: 1 cup butter; ¼ tsp. cloves; ½ cup sugar; 3 eggs (separated); ½ cup strawberry jam; 2 ½ cups flour; ½ cup strong black coffee; 1 tsp. soda dissolved in 4 tsp. sour cream; 1 tsp. cinnamon

Preheat oven to 350 degrees. Cream the butter and sugar thoroughly. Add jam and coffee mixed with spices. Beat egg yolks; blend with creamed mixture. Sift flour, add alternately with sour cream and soda mixture. Beat egg whites until stiff, then fold into mixture. Pour into 2 greased and floured 9" cake pans. Bake 45-55 minutes. Ice the cake with your favorite icing or whipped cream.

ﾘ

Graham Cracker Pie—Mrs. Theron Thompson Recipe

Crust: Use 12-16 crackers (roll fine). Mix with ½ cup melted butter and 1 tsp. flour and ½ cup sugar. Press into pie tin.

Custard: Heat 2 cups of milk. Separate yolks and whites of 3 eggs. Mix together: ¾ cup sugar and 2 tbsp. corn starch and pinch of salt. Beat egg yolks and stir above mixture into them. Cook mixture in the milk until it becomes thick. Pour into crust.

Meringue: Beat 3 whites of eggs with 3 tbsp. sugar and 1 tsp. baking powder. Put on custard. Bake pie for 15 minutes in 350 degree oven.

ﾘ

Oatmeal Cake—Contributed by Beverly Brown

Use: 2 cups (scant) boiling water; 1 ½ cups oats (uncooked); ¾ cup shortening; 1 ½ cup sugar; 1 ½ cups brown sugar (packed); 1 ½ tsp. vanilla; 3 eggs; 2 ¼ cups sifted flour; 1 ½ tsp. soda; ¾ tsp. salt; ¼ to ½ tsp. cinnamon; 1/3 tsp. nutmegCake Frosting—Use: ½ cup margarine (melted); ¾ cup brown sugar (packed); 2 ½ tbsp. milk or cream; ½ cup nutmeats; 1 cup coconut

Pour boiling water over oats, cover and let stand 20 minutes. Beat shortening until creamy, gradually add sugars and beat until fluffy. Blend in eggs and vanilla. Add oat mixture, mix well. Sift together flour, soda, salt, cinnamon and nutmeg. Add to creamed mixture. Mix well. Pour into greased and floured 9" x 13" pan and bake. (Do not remove cake from pan.) For the frosting, combine the ingredients and spread evenly over the baked cake. Broil until the frosting becomes bubbly, and watch carefully.

⌁

Fresh Apple Cake—Carol Shook Recipe

In a large bowl, cream: 1 ¼ sticks butter, 2 cups sugar, and 2 eggs (added one at a time).

Combine: 2 cups sifted flour, 2 cups raw apples (4-5), 1 cup raisins or dates, and 1 cup nuts.

Toss together in a large bowl (batter should be very dry and chunky).

Bake in a greased and floured pan (about 9"x13") at 350 degrees for 40-45 minutes. (For a 9"x 9" pan, bake for 50 minutes.)

⌁

Pantry Shop Cheese Slices (10-12 Servings)—Recipe by Mrs. Ann Zandall of Gary, Indiana

Use: 1 pkg. Red Star Active Dry Yeast; ¼ cup warm water; 1 tbsp. sugar; ½ cup Land O'Lakes Butter; 2 cups Pillsbury's Best All Purpose or Self-Rising Flour; 1 egg & ½ tsp. vanilla extract

Soften yeast in water. Combine sugar, butter, and flour in large mixer bowl, blending at low speed of mixer until mixture is the size of small peas. Add yeast, egg, and vanilla extract. Mix at low speed until a dough forms. Knead on lightly floured surface until smooth. Roll out two-thirds of dough to a 14 x 10 inch rectangle and remaining 1/3 of dough to a 12 x 8 inch rectangle for top crust. Place large rectangle in bottom of greased 12 x 8 inch pan, pulling dough up sides.

For filling use: 3 tbsp. plus ¾ cup sugar; 4 tbsp. flour; 1/8 tsp. salt; 13 ½ oz. can crushed pineapple (undrained); 2 eggs & 1 tsp. vanilla extract; 2 cups creamed small curd cottage cheese; 8 oz. pkg. cream cheese, softened; ½ cup flaked coconut

In small saucepan, combine 3 tbsp. sugar, 2 tbsp. flour, salt and pineapple. Cook over medium heat, stirring constantly, until thickened. Remove from heat and cool.

Beat eggs, vanilla extract and ¾ cup sugar in large mixer bowl at high speed of mixer until thick. Add cheeses, coconut and two tbsp. flour; beat at medium speed until well blended.

Prepare filling by spreading pineapple mixture on top of dough in pan. Carefully spread cheese mixture over pineapple mixture. Place top crust over filling. Fold bottom crust over top to seal edges. Cover, and let rise in warm place until light, about 1 hour. Flute edge. Bake at 375 degrees for 30-35 minutes. While warm, spread with Glaze. Refrigerate until time to serve.

Glaze—Combine 1 cup confectioners' sugar, 2 tbsp. milk, and ½ tsp. vanilla extract. Blend until smooth.

Encores of Fisherboy Memoirs, Book One

My first book in the Fisherboy Memoir Series was *Getting Hooked on Memoirs*, and the memoir receiving the most enthusiastic response was *My Pope Pius XII Photograph Session*. For that reason, I decided to bring it back for an encore in Book Two of the Fisherboy Series. Many memoirs from Book One could qualify as a close second in popularity, but I chose *The Baseball Glove That Had Two Thumbs* to be included for an encore. *My Evening with Robert Frost* might have been picked had another memoir been given encore status. Please read Book One to check on my choices.

My Pope Pius XII Photograph Session

On my first major tour of countries outside of the United States, I visited England and numerous countries on the European continent in 1957. Other than a single trip into Canada, I had never been outside the USA, and I had never had a flight in a plane. Perhaps my most memorable experience while on that tour of Europe was my photograph session with Pope Pius XII in the Vatican in May of 1957.

From early childhood, my family had always been Methodist, but my interest in singing religious music caused me to offer my services to many churches that were not Methodist. For many years, I was the choir soloist for my own Methodist church as well as the local Christian Science church, singing at each church every Sunday morning. Being a Methodist did nothing to lessen my expectation that my 1957 visit to the Vatican would be one of the highlights of my European tour, and this proved to be the case. In May of 1957, I arrived in Rome, nearing the end of my 46-day tour. The first sight that I visited was the Coliseum, which at one time was the entertainment center for ancient Rome where gladiators and lions engaged in mortal combat. That was followed by my visit to the Pantheon (the temple to "all the gods"), the Spanish Steps, and the Trevi Fountain. I recall tossing a number of liras into the fountain for good luck. Last, but not least, my attention was directed toward the Vatican.

As I stood in St. Peter's Square and looked at the Basilica, which dated back to 1614, I wondered if my "Trevi Fountain luck" would cause the Pope to make an appearance at his window high above the Square. True, he would have been several hundred yards away from me, but nonetheless, it would have allowed me to claim that I actually saw the Pope on my 1957 visit to Rome. Well, it was not to be, since he made no window appearance, but I later had a photograph session with Pope Pius XII. My explanation of this event with the Pope, though true, resembles the experiences of a fictional character such as Forrest Gump. After spending hours seeing the glories of the Sistine Chapel, I was passing through a very large room of the Vatican, and attendants suddenly rushed in and began using ropes to form a wide aisle. I moved forward and pressed my legs against the ropes, hoping that some noteworthy event was to take place shortly. Whatever the event, I would be positioned in the first row.

The room that had been nearly empty of visitors quickly filled to capacity. The crowd seemed to sense that some dignitary would appear, perhaps even Pope Pius XII. Shortly thereafter, four strong men entered through the door at the far side of the room carrying Pope Pius XII, seated in his elevated chair. The chair resembled a throne, and the Pope was regal in appearance, wearing the glasses usually seen in his photographs. He was perhaps a bit smaller than I would have expected, but he commanded everyone's attention. He wanted to be close to his subjects, and they wanted his touch and his blessing. The Pope was leaning far to his left side, attempting to reach the hands extended upward toward him, and I was positioned on that left side.

I had no doubt that the Pope was always welcomed enthusiastically by Catholics wherever he went, but on this occasion, he had an excited Methodist in his midst. This spiritual moment caused a surge in my emotions, as it must have for a woman standing some twenty rows behind me. This person was perhaps Catholic, because she did not hesitate to begin passing her baby over the heads of those in front of her, hoping the Pope would bless her baby as he passed by. The hands of at least twenty persons were needed to move the baby forward to the path followed by the Pope's procession. The baby suddenly came over my right shoulder and landed in my arms. Here I was with a baby I had never seen, and here came the Pope approaching me down the aisle. The Pope's attendants and his personal photographer were leading the procession.

An attendant came to my assistance, and the two of us held the baby high for the Pope to bless. The Pope's photographer apparently decided that this was a good photo opportunity, and he captured on film the Pope blessing the child. After the procession had passed my location, the photographer approached me, and he recorded my name and address. He promised that the picture just taken would be mailed to me. Within a matter of weeks, an envelope arrived from the Vatican containing the 8 x 11 inch black and white photograph. The baby was clearly the center of attention for the photographer's shot, but my profile was visible, and the photograph would remain as one of my most prized possessions. I did not see the Pope from St. Peter's Square that day in 1957, but I could prove that his photographer took our picture on that memorable day.

In closing this episode, I remind the reader that all of my memoirs are true. If you find it difficult to believe my account of the photograph session with the Pope, imagine how difficult it is for my wife to accept my explanation of the baby in the 1957 photograph. My wife and I first met in 1959, and we were married in 1960.

MARI, THE POPE'S PHOTOGRAPHER IN 2002

One evening in the year 2002, while watching television in my Westminster home, I chanced upon a documentary showing a day in the life of the "Pope's Photographer." The man snapping pictures was identified as Arturo Mari, and I hastily jotted down the name. I noted how the Pope's busy schedule in 2002 kept this energetic photographer on the run, and the photographer was often with the Pope from early morning until late at night. As I watched his typical day unfold, I naturally reflected on my experience in the Vatican in 1957, and I even began to imagine that this man resembled the photographer who took my picture in 1957. Questions were flying through my mind. *Could this be the same photographer that took my photograph?* and, *Why, after all of these years, would this man remind me of that 1957 photographer?* The answers to my questions were provided as the 2002 TV program came to a close.

The public television program announcements at the end of the program stunned me, because the announcer revealed that Arturo Mari was completing 45 years of service as the Pope's photographer. A quick subtraction of 45 from 2002 indicated that 1957 was his initial year of service, and that he was indeed the person that had taken my picture with Pope Pius XII in the Vatican. Perhaps my next action was risky, but I decided to mail the original 1957 photograph, with identifying stickers on the back, to the Vatican, hoping for some type of response. The envelope was addressed to "The Pope's Photographer," and I also enclosed a copy of my original memoir. Many of my friends said that the photographer would never see the material due to the massive amount of mail received by the Vatican. Their criticism of my poor judgment seemed to be valid, but then a response arrived from the Vatican.

The response I received from the Vatican was in the form of a large white envelope which returned the original photograph and nothing else. No letter or note was attached, and it was possible that Arturo had not actually read my letter or seen the 1957 picture. Weeks later, I reopened the envelope, and a closer look at the photograph revealed the photographer's signature near the bottom of the picture. Arturo's signature verified that he had, in fact, seen the picture, and he provided the proof that it was indeed his photograph, a picture that he had taken 45 years earlier in his first year as the "Pope's Photographer." I now knew that he had retained my letter and the memoir written about my 1957 visit to the Vatican. Now you know "The rest of the story!"

* Below is the August, 2002 Letter Sent To The Vatican *

To: Arturo Mari, Pope's
Photographer
Vatican City, Rome, Italy

Dear Sir:

At seventy-two years of age, I enjoy writing my memoirs and attaching photographs when available and when appropriate to the story. Enclosed is one of those interesting and humorous episodes. I believe that you may be part of that experience on May 19, 1957. The enclosed two pages and photograph tell the story. Several months ago, I was watching a public television station and the program placed great emphasis on the life of the Pope's Photographer in 2002. I was amazed to see that you resembled the Vatican photographer as I remembered him in 1957. Imagine my surprise when the speaker said that you were in your 45th year as the Pope's Photographer, and it appears that you came on the scene in 1957. Were you the one who snapped the enclosed photo and kindly mailed it to me? If yes, I would appreciate you autographing it before returning it to me in the self-addressed envelope.

I hope that you have fun reading my account of the 1957 incident and looking at what could have been one of your early photographs of Pope Pius XII. I also hope that you are the same person I met on my 1957 visit to the Vatican. In the 1957 picture, I am the well-hidden blonde directly behind the child, handing the girl in the white dress to the attendant. Thank you for considering my request. I look forward to your response.

Very sincerely, H. Kenneth Shook
301 Stoner Avenue, Westminster, MD USA 21157

OFFICIAL VATICAN RETURN ENVELOPE

ZIO FOTOGRAFICO

'OSSERVATORE ROMANO

20 CITTA' DEL VATICANO

06 698 84797 - Fax 06 698 84998
E-mail: photo@ossrom.va

3, 20

R 229582

CITTA' DEL VATICANO

DR H. KENNETH SHOOK
301 STONER AVE
WESTMINSTER, MD 21157
U. S. A.

'E - PRINTED MATTER

IEGARE - DO NOT BEND

Arturo Mari's 1957 original photo, unsigned

Arturo Mari's photo signed in 2002, 45 years later

THE BASEBALL GLOVE THAT HAD TWO THUMBS

[Conversations With Kelly & Greg Harris]

Perhaps it was in the late 1990s when the name of Greg Harris first came to my attention, and if what I heard was true, he had accomplished something never done by any other baseball player in the modern era of the Major Leagues. For this and other reasons, I thought how wonderful it would be to meet him and perhaps say, "Hello." He was an ambidextrous pitcher who actually made the big leagues, and, apparently, he pitched with both arms in the same inning of a Major League game. I began to gather bits and pieces of information about Greg Harris only to learn that two big league pitchers had the same name and played during some of the same years. The one that I wanted was Greg Allen Harris, born November 2, 1955, and he played in the Majors from 1981 to 1995.

A bit of searching, combined with a bit of luck, produced a phone number and an address which could possibly have been those belonging to "my Greg Harris." If I was correct, I could call him in California and say "This is Ken Shook calling from Maryland," but for weeks, I could not build up the nerve to make the call. I did have unlimited long-distance phone service, so cost was not an issue. What concerned me was the fact that there seemed to be little justification for Greg to share any part of his valuable time with me on the phone. One night at about 11:30 PM, I got the nerve I needed. I jumped out of bed and quickly dialed the California number before losing my nerve. The number actually rang a few times and then gave out a high pitched tone. To me, this meant the line was out of service. (Others later reminded me it could have been the phone's signal for receiving a FAX.) The next day, I decided to mail a package to the address in my notes, explaining my interest in Greg's accomplishments and stating my interest in writing memoirs. The next week, to my utter delight and surprise, a call came to my home from Kelly Harris, Greg's wife.

Kelly Harris related that Greg was on the road with the college team he coached, but that he wanted to talk with me when he returned home on Friday. She said I could call at 11:00 Maryland time. I thought she meant at night, but she clarified she was suggesting a morning call, which would be 8:00 AM California time. It seems that my mailed material arrived at the home of Greg's parents, and when passed along, both Kelly and Greg liked what I had written. One item I had included was a song, *"My Pre-Game Routine."* Greg was interested that Cal Ripken, Jr., had written to me about the song's lyrics, and Kelly said that Greg wanted me to sing the song to him. Kelly and I talked for nearly an hour, and she was perfectly delightful.

Kelly Harris was understandably enthusiastic about her husband's remarkable baseball accomplishments and insisted that he belonged in the Hall of Fame. This former runner-up to a "Miss California" title said that she and Greg had only been married for the past two years, but that many years earlier, they had been high school sweethearts. The missing years were not discussed, but Greg had married another person, and they had a number of children before that marriage ended in divorce. Kelly showed her sympathy for the first wife by saying that someone should write about the amount of stress placed on the families of many professional baseball players, especially the wives. Before ending our phone conversation, Kelly encouraged me to ask Greg about certain experiences that she knew were important to him (like his trip to Alaska to play summer ball), and she also asked me: "What's a curve ball, exactly?" I laughed at her question, and it made me appreciate how honest and open she was as a person. Greg was a lucky fellow to have found Kelly a second time.

Before calling Greg on Friday, April 10, 2009, I jotted down some of the information that had stayed with me from numerous sources. I remembered that he had been the property of nine different teams during his 15 year Major League career, and with some effort I could name them. They were the New York Mets, Cincinnati Reds, San Diego Padres, Texas Rangers, Cleveland Indians, Philadelphia Phillies, Boston Red Sox, New York Yankees, and Montreal Expos. With all of these moves, Kelly's concern about the resulting stress on Greg's first marriage was understandable. Basic stats were available on Greg's playing days, but I came up with some interesting calculations of my own, and all were to Greg's credit. The batters facing him over his fifteen years in the big leagues must have had an average of no more than .235, and Greg had recorded a strike-out for every 4-5 batters he faced. He only averaged one walk in ten batters faced, and some of those walks must have been intentional. Considering that Greg was fully capable of throwing with both arms for most of the fifteen years he played in the Majors and considering that being ambidextrous has been his apparent claim to fame, it is startling to find that of the more than 6,000 batters faced in his big league career, he threw left-handed to only two of those batters. He wore his famous glove the day he faced those two batters, the glove that he designed with four fingers and two thumbs, a glove capable of being worn on either hand.

My Friday 8:00 AM phone call was answered in California by Kelly, and she called Greg to the phone. Greg and I chatted for a while without the conversation going in any special direction, and it seemed that Greg expected to respond to a series of questions that I had prepared. Before questioning Greg, I decided to first share some of my own baseball experiences, and he seemed genuinely interested in hearing them. I mentioned that I had actually batted against an ambidextrous pitcher in a high school game in 1948, and I could not imagine any athletic feat to be more difficult in all of sports than a pitcher throwing with both arms. The idea that someone would do it at the Major League level was unthinkable, in my opinion.

In one other experience, I recalled using the smallest bat I could find against the best fast-ball pitcher in the Maryland State Baseball League. By not using my usual Rogers Hornsby style bat, my swing was quicker, allowing me to hit a home run off Harvey McCutchin. On my next trip to the plate, Harvey evened the score by throwing his first pitch at my head. He missed my head, but the toss did break a bone in my hand and I was out for the rest of that season. Greg said that he knew two of my former baseball coaches, Jim Boyer (a former big league umpire) and Mule Haas (a former star player for the Philadelphia Athletics). Like Greg, I too had a special ball glove. Mine was a three-pronged mitt for use at first base. I bought it in 1944, the same year that I met 16 year old Nellie Fox. Nellie was a rookie at the 1944 Athletics' training camp in my home town of Frederick, MD, and his efforts to play first base for the Athletics would not be rewarded. As stated elsewhere, his first baseman's glove would never make it to the Baseball Hall of Fame, but Nellie would make the Hall as a star second baseman for the Chicago White Sox.

My first question for Greg asked how he got started pitching with both arms. Had his father or a coach suggested that he give it a try? Greg said, "No!" to both questions. It was something he felt comfortable doing, and he stayed with it even though those around him generally frowned on the effort. Greg was so successful in his early years of baseball that he was offered contracts by big league teams in 1974, 1975, and 1976. He thought he was ready to play at the higher levels, but those around him talked him into rejecting all three offers. In the summer of 1976, the offers he longed for suddenly disappeared, so he journeyed to Alaska to play in a summer league especially designed for college ball players seeking recognition. Greg and his team won many awards that summer, and Greg accepted one of his end-of-summer contract offers. He signed with the New York Mets in September of 1976 and his pro career was underway.

Greg surprised me when he said that he did not throw his first curve ball until the age of seventeen. In his earlier years, he relied solely on his fast ball and his changeup to have great success on the mound. Without a curve ball there would have been little motivation for a pitcher to attempt to throw with both arms. Greg shared with me his test for judging a pitcher's readiness to pitch with the second arm. Greg's second arm was his left, and he could meet all three requirements he had established in the test: 1) pitches had to exceed 80 miles per hour in velocity; 2) pitch selections had to include an effective curve ball; and 3) out of 35 pitches thrown to the plate, at least 30 had to be in the strike zone. I responded by saying to Greg that many big league pitchers today could not meet the third requirement even with their number one arm.

I wanted to hear more about his unique pitcher's glove. Greg said he designed it, and he had a recognized company produce it. He said he still had a number of the gloves safely stored in his home at the time of our phone conversation. The glove he designed had four fingers and a thumb on each end, allowing the glove to be worn on either hand. During team practices, he often ran and caught flies in the outfield, and during these times he said he wore the glove on his right hand, throwing with his left arm. Greg never mentioned throwing batting practice left-handed, but if his coaches saw him doing it, they would most likely have stopped the action at once. Greg said his glove violated no Major League rules, and he in fact used such a glove in his history-making 1995 game against the Cincinnati Reds.

I knew there would be humor connected to his description of the time he hurt his elbow throwing sunflower seeds into the stands from the dugout. I asked: "Is it true that you actually hurt your elbow in this way?" "Yes!" was his quick response. I said that his coaches would naturally be upset with what some might call rather juvenile behavior, but even his father no doubt expressed displeasure with him. Greg said his father said nothing about the incident but rather sent him a package. "What was in the package?" I asked. Greg replied that his father had sent him a slingshot to use for future sunflower tosses into the stands.

Greg's longest stay with a team had been his five seasons with the Boston Red Sox. He played for them in 1990, 1991, 1992, 1993 and 1994. The next highest number of seasons spent with a team was 1985, 1986, and 1987, the years spent with the Texas Rangers. At Boston, the coaches were pleased with Greg's right-handed throwing, but never gave his left arm any serious consideration. I had heard that Greg sometimes wore his special glove to show his displeasure with the coaches decisions. When asked about it, Greg would not admit that any friction existed between himself and the coaches. Days after my phone conversation with Greg, I came across a picture of Greg in a Boston Red Sox uniform, and he was on the mound throwing with his left arm while wearing his special glove. If not intended to irritate the team coaches and management, why else would such a picture have been taken? Perhaps the photo proves that Greg had a great sense of humor, because during his entire five seasons with Boston, Greg had never thrown a single pitch to a batter with his left arm. Also, it appears he signed the card *Cy Harris,* perhaps comparing himself to the immortal baseball pitcher, Cy Young.

Greg was willing to describe the inning in which his life-long dream was finally realized. His Montreal team worked it out that he would be allowed to use both arms in pitching one of the final games of the 1995 season. He expected to enter that game earlier, but his appearance was limited to Cincinnati's last inning at bat. After a brief warm up of his right arm (he was not allowed to warm up both arms), he faced Reggie Sanders and got the right-handed hitter to ground out to the shortstop. Next came two left-handed hitters, Hal Morris and Ed Trubensee. Greg turned his back to home plate and returning to the mound with his glove now on his right hand. The batter and the umpire had to have been shocked to see Greg prepare to throw left-handed. Having had no warm up tosses with the left arm, Greg was wild and threw one pitch all the way to the backstop. He walked Hal before getting Ed to ground out. Since the next batter was right-handed hitter Bret Boone, Greg again switched the glove, this time to his left hand, and he retired the final batter on another weak infield roller back to the mound. The game ended and Greg had accomplished something never before done in the modern era of Major League baseball, pitching with both arms in a big league ball game. Greg's dream was finally realized.

Did Greg's achievement bring him the attention that it seemed to merit? Perhaps not! Greg reasoned that his playing for Montreal was the cause of the lack of interest in the event. Had he been pitching for a team in this country rather than a team in Canada, the news media may have given the event more coverage. The most noteworthy phone call to his home the next day was from the baseball Hall of Fame. This call, requesting something like a signed game ball for the museum, came as no surprise to Greg. He was happy to honor their request, but he suggested that he give them a different item to commemorate his unique accomplishment. The Hall of Fame welcomed Greg's gift suggestion, which was his pitcher's glove with four fingers and two thumbs.

Greg's impact on Major League baseball has required rules committees to focus greater attention on the rules governing switch-hitters and switch-pitchers. Just what is an ambidextrous pitcher allowed to do and not do? How often should a switch-batter be allowed to position himself on different sides of home plate? Greg said that current rules require a pitcher to stay with the same arm used on his first pitch to a batter, and a switch-hitter can change sides of the plate only until he has received a count of two strikes. I mentioned that there seems to be some debate about a switch-pitcher facing a switch-batter, and the question is: Who must first indicate his intensions?

The batter wants the pitcher to indicate which arm he will use, and the pitcher wants to know the batter's position at the plate. It was Greg's opinion that rules generally are aimed to protect and favor the hitters rather than the pitchers, and if Greg is correct, this suggests that baseball fans prefer to see high scoring games rather than see pitchers throw no-hitters.

Greg retired from big league play after the 1995 season, and, as any movie script would have it, his lifelong dream was realized just prior to the close of that last season. Greg continues to contribute to the sport of baseball by coaching college-age players, and perhaps his love for switch-pitching and switch-hitting will rub off on some of them. The life of Kelly and Greg Harris is worthy of a movie in my opinion, and while they are both still young at heart and young in appearance, I feel that they should be allowed to play the lead roles in the film. I'd be willing to be an extra in such a film. If the movie's director allowed that to happen, I'd like to be seated in the stands next to Greg's dad, and we could catch sunflower seeds that might be thrown our way from the dugout.

Greg Harris   Kelly Harris

ABOUT THE AUTHOR

Dr. Ken Shook, pictured with Shadow, served as a  college dean of admissions for 18 years and ran the Maryland State Scholarship Board for 10 years. He wants everyone to write their memoirs. He has been sharing his love for memoirs with others for many years, conducting workshops and lecturing to groups in the middle-Atlantic area. His annual appearances at the Random House Bookfair in Westminster, Maryland, are well received.

Dr. Shook has two memoir collections, *Getting Hooked On Memoirs* and *Family Cars Trigger Memoirs,* and asks you to write your memoirs by thinking small. He has also edited two memoir collections, one for the 1952 graduating class of Western Maryland College and another for the 1958 graduates of Madison High School (NJ). Numerous education articles have been printed in the NACAC Journal and The College Board Review, and his collection of Rotary songs has been at the top of Google search lists for many years. Ken, wife Carol, and Shadow have their residence in Westminster, Maryland.

Fisherboy Memoir Series, Book Two

"What a lovely cover! Congratulations on this publication." 8/24/11 Suzanna Tamminen, Director—Wesleyan University Press

"I love your piece about the Methodist boy holding a baby for the Pope" and related to the memoir *The baseball glove that had two thumbs*, "It's warm and unusual material, very American." William Zinsser, Author and Educator

Family Cars Trigger Memoirs presents both a guide and a collection of memoirs designed to provide examples of this personal type of writing. In this helpful handbook, Dr. Shook offers practical advice to aid in writing effective personal memoirs, and he draws on his numerous experiences in conducting sessions on writing and sharing memoirs. This practical guide will inspire all who reads it to delve into their own life experiences to share their stories and true life experiences in their very own memoirs.

Ken Shook and his dog, Shadow, will welcome you to his web site at: kenshookmemoirs.com